700 North Adams Street

7⁰⁰ North Adams Street

THE FLORIDA GOVERNOR'S MANSION FOUNDATION
TALLAHASSEE ❧ FLORIDA

EDITOR IN CHIEF   *Rhea Chiles*

MANAGING EDITOR   *Kimbel Orr*

DESIGNER   *Denise Choppin*

PHOTOGRAPHER   *Ray Stanyard*

WRITERS   *Dennis Gephardt*
            Lacy Bullard

Published by

**The Florida Governor's Mansion
F O U N D A T I O N**

700 North Adams Street
Tallahassee, Florida 32303

Printed in Hong Kong

Library of Congress
Catalog Number: 96-078423

ISBN: 0-9654772-0-7

700 NORTH ADAMS STREET

is dedicated to the preservation

of the cultural heritage

of all Floridians.

$\mathcal{U}$NDERWRITERS

The Florida Governor's Mansion Foundation
gratefully acknowledges those who have
provided the funds to create and publish

700 $\mathcal{N}$ORTH $\mathcal{A}$DAMS $\mathcal{S}$TREET

The Law Firms of Anderson & Orcutt, P.A. and Hobby Anderson & Grey

Beneficial Management Corporation of America

Mr. and Mrs. Michael Bienes

Mr. and Mrs. William Bours Bond

Mr. and Mrs. A. Worley Brown

Mr. and Mrs. Joseph F. Chapman III

Rhea and Lawton Chiles

The Carl S. Swisher Foundation, Inc.

Mr. Steve Del Gallo

Florida Power & Light Company

Florida Rock Industries, Inc.

Mr. and Mrs. Ben Hill Griffin III

NDERWRITERS

Mr. Richard J. Herman, Harbor Branch Oceanographic Institution, Inc.

Mr. and Mrs. Winston K. Howell, Thomas Howell Ferguson P.A.

Mr. and Mrs. Kenneth Kirchman

Mr. and Mrs. Carlton D. Lewis

Mr. and Mrs. Eduardo A. Masferrer, Hamilton Bank, N.A.

Mr. and Mrs. Kirk McKay, Jr.

Dr. and Mrs. Salomon E. Melgen

Mr. and Mrs. T. Wainwright Miller, The John E. and Aliese Price Foundation

Mrs. Kathryn Mills

Mr. Richard P. Morette

Dr. and Mrs. Michael Patipa

Jim and Alexis Pugh

Dr. and Mrs. Steven M. Scott

Dr. and Mrs. José Serra

Mr. and Mrs. A. M. Shuler

Sprint

Mr. and Mrs. Thomas W. Staed

The Liz Whitney Tippett Foundation

TABLE OF CONTENTS

INTRODUCTION   **11**

**A CENTURY
OF CHANGE**   **12**

OPEN HOUSE   **36**

The State Rooms   *42*

The Family Rooms   *76*

Gardens & Grounds   *84*

**FIRST FAMILIES
AT HOME**   **100**

THE MANSION COMMISSION AND
FOUNDATION TRUSTEES   141

ACKNOWLEDGMENTS   142

SELECTED BIBLIOGRAPHY AND
ARCHIVAL PHOTOGRAPHY   143

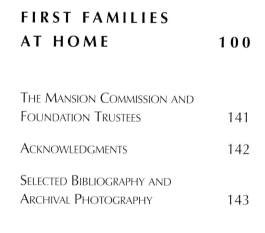

Introduction

Few visitors to Tallahassee see the Florida Governor's Mansion immediately. It is not located among the white office buildings clustered around the tower of the Capitol on its hilltop. Those who seek it find pleasant gardens surprisingly close to the bustle of state business, but a world away in feeling. They find a welcoming house, under the shade of live oaks, on a site chosen by legislators when the twentieth century was young. There are many larger houses, older houses, more opulent houses in Florida, but for Floridians, the Governor's Mansion represents the state in a way no other house can.

These pages convey the changes of nearly ninety years on this historic site. In the present house and in the one which preceded it, twenty-three governors and their families have lived through the light and shadows of history. Since the first official residence was occupied in 1907, the grounds have known both a carriage house and a garage, a chicken coop and a swimming pool. World War II and the cold war cast shadows here, a blackout room was added, later a fallout shelter was built. The laughter of children, the pleasure of pets, occasions of family joy, and darker times of family tragedy — all are here. The rooms shown in these photographs and the objects that furnish them, as well as the gardens and the outdoor areas, represent a part of every Floridian's heritage. That they are lovely and gracious should make each Floridian proud.

A CENTURY OF CHANGE

Celebrated authors have written hundreds of volumes about Florida — about its natural resources, settlements, commerce, and the political and military struggles that have shaped its history. This story involves just two homes in Florida — but unique homes. It is the story of the events and people that shaped the character of Florida's two governor's mansions.

From the time that Spanish explorer Juan Ponce de Leon landed in Florida in 1513, until statehood in 1845, some eighty-two men served the governments of Spain, England and the United States as governors of the lands now known as Florida. For most of those years St. Augustine and Pensacola were the colonial capital cities, and the quarters that housed the governors were relatively simple structures. They usually crouched inside fortified walls, protected by armed garrisons.

Since 1907 the state of Florida has provided its chief with a governor's mansion on North Adams Street in Tallahassee. The residences on the site have offered thousands of visitors from the state, the nation and around the world an opportunity to celebrate the mansion's heritage and enjoy the hospitality of its residents. Designed and built by Floridians, both structures reveal the aspirations of their creators.

In 1824, Florida's territorial governor William P. DuVal announced that Tallahassee would become the seat of government of the new U.S. territory. For the next eight decades, Florida's chief executives provided their own housing in the small town. When Florida entered the twentieth century, bristling with energy and rising in national image, some citizens believed the time had come to provide their chief with a suitable home. The *Florida Metropolis*, a Jacksonville newspaper, described the predicament of Florida's governors in its issue of March 25, 1903: "Since the Governor receives but $3,500 per year, he must do the best he can at boarding houses and hotels, precluding proper social functions expected of a head of state." Governor William Jennings proposed to the 1903 Florida legislature that they appropriate $30,000 to fund the building of an official residence. The vote ended in controversy over where the residence should be located, and the issue simmered without resolution for the next two years.

In 1905, the sixtieth year of statehood, the legislature appropriated $25,000 to build an executive residence for the governor in an act that provided "for the Acquisition of a Site, and the Erection, Building and Furnishing of a Mansion Thereon for the Governor of the State of Florida." The act also created the Florida Governor's Mansion Commission composed of

PAGE 12: **Florida's first governor's mansion arose from the raw north Florida landscape. This watercolor depicts the neoclassical building soon after its completion. The architectural design of the mansion gave form to a vision brimming with the aspirations of Floridians at the turn of the twentieth century.**

An unknown English artist produced this *View of the Governor's House* in St. Augustine in 1764. Made of local coquina, or shellrock, the walls of the home were twenty-two inches thick and designed to outlast previous wooden structures.

After Florida achieved statehood in 1845, Governor William D. Moseley (1795–1863) ordered a new state seal made. This glass version of the first seal hung in the ceiling of the United States House of Representatives from 1857 until 1951 when it was given to the state. It is housed in the Museum of Florida History in Tallahassee.

A French visitor, Francis de la Porte, Comte de Castelnau, depicted the capitol in 1838. He noted, "The building in which the territorial Assembly meets bears the imposing name of capitol. The structure is built of wood in the midst of a sort of very pretty little grove forming a park with a charming effect near the middle of the city." Of the men who met in the building, he wrote "… most of them are planters and farmers, but as elsewhere, lawyers also exert their influence in them."

This detail from an 1885 lithograph offers a *View of the City of Tallahassee* in an era when governors had to arrange for their own housing. The official executive residence would come twenty-two years later.

The mansion site was once part of property originally owned by two-time territorial governor Richard Keith Call.

Florida's chief executives had to provide their own housing prior to 1907. During his terms as governor, William D. Bloxham (1835–1911) lived in this house at 410 North Calhoun Street. Built in the 1830s, it is Tallahassee's only surviving Federal style townhouse.

the governor, the comptroller and three citizens. The legislators suggested Jackson Square as a site for the commission to consider. The city of Tallahassee owned this choice tract of land southeast of the capitol, but city officials declined to part with it on the grounds that they could not legally convey it to the state. The act also stated that if there were no suitable public lands available, the allotted funds could not be used to purchase a privately owned site. Instead, private land would have to be donated to the state. When the options for procuring land seemed to be running out, George Saxon, a Tallahassee banker, generously conveyed to the state four lots presently addressed as 700 North Adams Street, on the northern city limits of Tallahassee.

With the deed to the property in hand, the commission turned its attention to the selection of an architect. They chose the man who had helped Jacksonville lift itself from the ashes of the devastating fire of 1901, Henry John Klutho. Klutho's neoclassical plan for the governor's mansion recalled the ancient roots of Florida's democratic traditions. Twenty-four Ionic columns with elaborate capitals vaulted from the front portico floor to the architrave. The [Tallahassee] *Weekly True Democrat* described Klutho's design as follows: "In these plans the proposed building presents a very handsome

appearance outwardly. The front and sides are surrounded by a broad gallery supported by massive columns to the height of the building. The plans include arrangements for a furnace for heating, numerous baths, and all modern conveniences." The colonnaded porte cochère added to the scale of the impressive exterior which surrounded the relatively modest structure.

On the main level the interior organization was Georgian in style with formal rooms arranged around a central passage. Pocket doors allowed the rooms to merge for large receptions. The second floor provided bedrooms and baths for the family. The unfinished attic allowed for storage and future expansion.

The commission quickly turned their attention to selecting a construction company. After screening the bids of four construction companies, they selected local builder Orion C. Parker. The *Weekly True Democrat* reported on the remarkably peaceful and relatively short negotiations: "The Mansion Commission was delighted that the building was let without the usual amount of annoyances encountered, such as postponements, private sessions, etc. The whole matter was closed in three hours and left for the architect and the builder to put up the building." Horse-drawn lorries carried the wooden columns to the site as Parker's workmen labored from dawn until dusk. Townsfolk came to watch

Florida's first member of the American Institute of Architects, Henry John Klutho (1873–1964), designed the original mansion. The second-generation German-American developed his graphic skills while attending a drawing academy in Missouri, and working with professional architects. He continued his education in New York City and studied architectural masterpieces of the Old World during an extended tour of Europe. He moved to Jacksonville in 1901. A friend of architect Frank Lloyd Wright, Klutho became an early advocate for Prairie School design in the southeast. Many of his buildings, both public and private, still remain in Florida.

Sons of the mansion's builder, Orion and Robert, ride astride a horse-drawn column making its way to the work site. Robert Parker later served as mayor of Tallahassee from 1949 to 1950.

Wearing his signature bowler, Orion C. Parker and his crew pause for a photo showing the progress at the site. The *Tallahassee True Democrat* reported on August 10, 1906: "The building is as yet incomplete. From what stands there — its broad front and many windows — it is to be undoubtedly a noble structure, fitted exactly for this clime and its purpose."

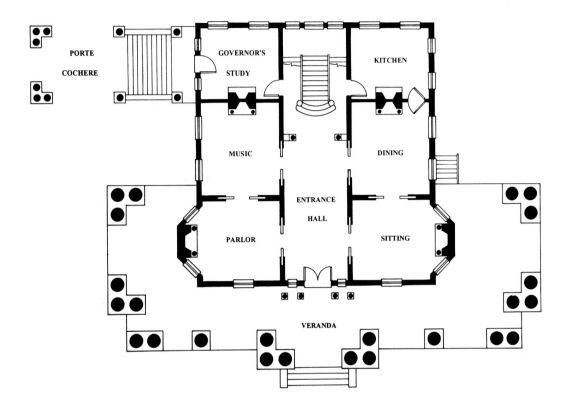

PORTE

COCHERE

GOVERNOR'S

STUDY

KITCHEN

MUSIC

DINING

ENTRANCE

HALL

PARLOR

SITTING

VERANDA

John Henry Klutho, Jacksonville architect, believed that a tasteful public building reflected the education and refinement of its citizens. His plan for the ground floor of the original mansion featured a central hall leading to the formal rooms of the house, each with a fireplace. This plan clearly shows the generous verandah which enhanced the scale of the building.

the historic work in progress and marveled at the emergence of the architectural grandeur.

*L*iving in a nearby rented house on Monroe Street, the family of Governor Napoleon Broward observed the progress with particular interest. First Lady Annie Isabell Douglass Broward busied herself with plans to furnish the fourteen rooms of the mansion with $4,444.75 allotted by the legislature. The *Weekly True Democrat* reported on her achievement: "What is here is very handsome, most of it being solid mahogany, upholstered in green. ... Altogether there is a promise of a very tasteful and pleasing interior when all the furniture is placed and the various ornaments arranged." Lawmakers also appropriated funds to landscape the mansion grounds and purchase two lots that adjoined the mansion property. In May of 1907, even though the house was incomplete, the Browards hosted a legislative reception. Guests made their way down a receiving line in the front drawing room decorated with Florida greenery of smilax and ferns. The *Weekly True Democrat* covered the housewarming: "Music was furnished by an orchestra seated in the front balcony on the second floor, and punch [was] served in the dining room by several of our most popular and charming ladies." Four months later Governor Broward and his family stepped over the threshold to occupy the newly completed mansion.

The dramatic double-return staircase in the original mansion split to two sets of stairs above the landing, where a six-paneled stained glass window in the art nouveau style refracted western sunlight.

Governor Albert Gilchrist and three guests are reflected in the beveled mirror of an eclectic hatrack which offered artificial light as well as a deeply upholstered bench. Gilchrist served from 1909 to 1913, and this view of the ground floor reveals the cluttered look popular at the time. The parlor and music room opened from the south side of the hall.

A group of children and puppies stay still just long enough to be captured by a panoramic camera in front of the governor's mansion in the 1930s. Adams Street remained unpaved at its northern end, but pedestrians enjoyed a wide sidewalk in the evolving neighborhood.

Decorated for the inauguration of Fuller Warren on January 4, 1949, the mansion, with its imposing scale, dwarves two young Floridians waiting on the front steps.

This photo, taken from the stairwell during a 1947 legislative reception hosted by Governor and Mrs. Millard Caldwell, reveals the crowded conditions which occurred on the main floor.

Each of the fifteen families who lived in the first mansion expressed their individual lifestyles. Writing in 1953, Grace Wing of the *Miami Daily News* described this passage of time: "The mellow old Mansion ... has the charm and imagination appeal of any home that has shared the struggles and triumphs of those who have lived in it through the years." In the early days it was not uncommon to see cows grazing on the lawn or, as late as the 1940s, to hear chickens clucking at the rear of the property. After the addition of a circular driveway, the grounds became a favorite roller-skating spot for neighborhood children. For formal evening events the mood would be transformed as guests arrived. The house became a popular show place on the itinerary of Tallahassee visitors who could purchase postcards of the impressive verandah with its white colonnade. As the years went by, modifications to the building reflected the changing times. During World War II the attic was upgraded as part of a plan to provide a blackout room in case of enemy air raids. In response to the need for additional space, workers added lean-to additions on the rear side of the building.

*W*hen Parker built the first mansion, it was just outside the city limits, but by the mid-twentieth century, as Tallahassee grew, residential and commercial development surrounded the property. Across the 100-foot wide Adams Street, four houses fronted the mansion, including the home of Robert A. Gray, secretary of state from 1930 to 1961. After the establishment of an executive residence in 1907, Florida experienced a phenomenal population growth. In his *Florida Handbook* of 1949–1950, Allen Morris described a shortcoming of the building: "The Governor's Mansion is lacking in the rooms in which great receptions might be held. ... The great growth and importance of not only Tallahassee but of the State was not anticipated and the plans were for the accommodation of small parties. . . ." Guests at crowded mansion gatherings began to murmur about their discomfort in the cramped quarters, and first families grumbled about the increasing deterioration of living conditions in the house. Increasing demands on the mansion exposed the limitations of its turn-of-the-century design: the dining room seated only twelve guests, the reception area was too small and the family had no private living area. Finally, doubts as to its structural integrity set the stage for a dramatic sequence of events that shook the mansion to its very foundations.

In a pique and desperate, Governor Fuller Warren labeled the mansion "The State Shack." At a public cabinet meeting in 1949, he bewailed, "I've had to move my bed two or three times to keep plaster from falling on the occupant." In a 1952 letter to the legislature, Warren advanced his cause: "I further recommend a sum of money to be appropriated sufficient to build an adequate residence for Florida's Chief Executive. The Executive Mansion is nearly fifty years old and in dilapidated condition. Its chimneys have been condemned as unsafe for use. … It is not believed that repairs can put the Mansion in condition adequate and safe for human habitation."

*N*o sooner had the 1953 legislature responded to the increasing hue and cry for action by appropriating $250,000 to build a new mansion, than a dispute erupted between the house and senate over where the new mansion would be built. Senate proponents of the existing in-town site proclaimed that the governor did not have time to be a "country squire" and needed a work and meeting place close to the capitol. Members of the house, however, wanted a suburban site. Neither side would give an inch.

To break the impasse, the legislature directed the governor and the cabinet to make the decision, placing the responsibility for site selection on the shoulders of newly elected Governor Dan McCarty. Although of the opinion that the new mansion should remain in the location it had historically occupied, McCarty was willing to go along with recommendations made by a

On July 27, 1955, Howard Cranston auctioned most of the furnishings from the old mansion to clear it for demolition. Strings of lights illuminated the front lawn during the sale, which stretched past midnight. The proceeds were used toward furnishing the new building. The *Tallahassee Democrat* reported:

"From the wide front door, through which thousands of people have passed in gala attire for state receptions, came a steady stream of workmen carrying chairs, sofas, bedspreads, rugs, draperies, mattress pads, firescreens and silver pieces."

Auctioneer Cranston extolled the virtues of "Item 145, a love seat from the second floor northeast bedroom," while workers moved it to the porch. The love seat fetched $37.50.

study committee which he appointed. While some members of his committee argued for maintaining the current location, others were adamant in their belief that the mansion should be moved to the outskirts of the city.

A correspondent for the *St. Petersburg Times* defined the debate: "Chief argument against moving the Mansion is the historical value of the present site. Arguments for moving are that Tallahassee's business district is pushing north and gradually crowding the Mansion. Actually, the business district now is only one block away, and there is little room for parking for large functions."

The confrontation escalated beyond the question of where to locate the new mansion to "Why raze the existing mansion in the first place?" Conflicting engineering reports on the fitness of the mansion only served to widen the chasm separating the two sides.

In 1955, newly inaugurated Governor LeRoy Collins and the cabinet decided to exercise their lawful authority to settle this matter. They boldly stepped forward with their verdict: demolish the old mansion and build a new one on the same site. Legislators who opposed this edict framed their argument with a new twist: preserve the old mansion as a museum. A last-minute resolution was introduced which stated:

"It is the opinion of the members of the Legislature that the present governor's mansion should be preserved for its historical value." The local chapter of the United Daughters of the Confederacy gave its unanimous support to the preservation of the existing governor's mansion. However, the decision to demolish the old and build anew had a clear majority in the legislature, and plans to demolish the old mansion continued.

On July 8, 1955, auctioneer Howard Cranston conducted a bidding session for salvage rights to the mansion. The twenty-five minute sale began with the playing of Rosemary Clooney's 1955 hit "This Ole House." The record player on the front porch sang out:

> This old house is getting shaky
> This old house is getting old
> This old house once rang with laughter
> This old house heard many shouts.
> Now it trembles in the darkness
> As the lightning walks about.

A CBS television camera recorded Governor Collins as he stood and spoke about the "rather sad occasion." He said, "We hate to see the old house go. As houses go, it's not really very old, but many of us had hoped it could be saved." He unveiled the plans for the new mansion and

P. L. Burkhalter, Sr., of Jacksonville won the bid to clear the site. His wrecking company sold architectural remnants of the building as it came down in 1955. The twenty-four Ionic columns remained in their stately configuration as the demolition progressed.

By December 1955 the lot was cleared and ready for construction to begin on the new building. The old fence remained marking the boundary of the work area.

explained that his family would be moving next door to the Grove, an antebellum home built by Richard Keith Call, territorial governor and great-grandfather of First Lady Mary Call Collins.

The P. L. Burkhalter Wrecking Company of Jacksonville made the winning bid of $900 to clear the site, dig out the foundation and retain rights to all salvageable building material. Before demolition could begin, the Florida Governor's Mansion Advisory Committee requested that the furnishings inside the mansion be auctioned as well. Howard Cranston's men installed strings of lights overhead in anticipation of the sale going well into the night of July 27, 1955. Folding chairs covered the front lawn for the expected large crowd. The *Tallahassee Democrat* informed its readers: "At 6 p.m. tomorrow Howard Cranston will take up his position on the front steps and offer for sale the first item in a list of furnishings which includes almost everything used by governors in the past 50 years." The household furnishings and goods were displayed for public inspection, and refreshments were available to slake thirsts aggravated by the heat. When all items had been auctioned, proceeds of the sale amounted to $7,500.

The family of Governor Collins, along with members of the mansion household staff, settled

Architect Marion Sims Wyeth (1889–1982) was born in Brooklyn, New York. His family had roots in both South Carolina and Alabama, and he considered himself a southerner. Wyeth studied, however, far from the south — at Princeton University and at the Ecole des Beaux-Arts in Paris. In 1919 when Wyeth began to work in Palm Beach, noted architect Addison Mizner offered to hire him. Wyeth declined the offer and instead started his own firm. Influenced by his classical training, Wyeth's designs for private Palm Beach homes delighted his well-to-do clientele. At ninety-two, Wyeth reflected on the difficulty of pleasing so many parties with his governor's mansion design. "It served a dual purpose," he explained. "It had to be formal and livable too. It was the hardest plan to conceive." He remembered it as his best job.

into the Grove, which served as the semiofficial executive residence while the new mansion was being constructed. A *Tampa Tribune* writer explained, "While the new Governor's Mansion is under construction, Mary Call Collins still must manage a household befitting her husband's official position as Florida's highest official. With charm and graciousness she presides over her own home, The Grove — only a stone's throw from the Mansion site."

The Burkhalters set about dismantling the forty-eight-year-old governor's mansion. During demolition a crane lowered the twenty-four Ionic columns from their stately configuration. By December the site stood clear.

Cabinet members and spouses, along with the Governor's Mansion Advisory Council, selected Marion Sims Wyeth as the architect who could best tailor the new mansion to suit the chief executive of a state rising to national prominence. A widely acclaimed Palm Beach architect, the sixty-seven-year-old Wyeth had an excellent reputation for designing palatial homes in south Florida. A relative of famed American painter Andrew Wyeth, he was also known to employ a cost-conscious spirit when designing for public projects. As instructed, Wyeth used the Hermitage, the Tennessee home of President Andrew Jackson, as his exterior

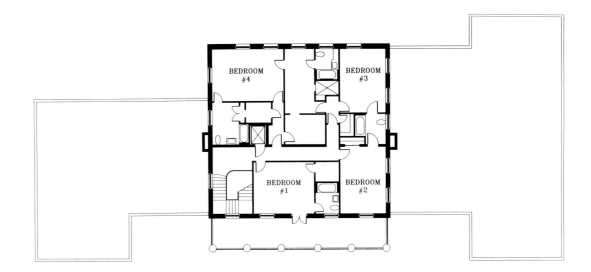

SECOND FLOOR

FIRST FLOOR

LEFT: Marion Sims Wyeth's plans for the residence included separate state rooms and family areas on the first and second floors. Experienced in the design of homes for entertaining, he called for a large kitchen between the two dining rooms. These plans show the house after the 1985 addition of the Florida room.

In June of 1956, Governor and Mrs. LeRoy Collins reviewed progress at the site with Tallahassee builder J. O. Carlile. The cast stone columns were crafted in south Florida and then trucked to Tallahassee.

model. Like that of the Hermitage, the facade of the mansion is comprised of a two-story center section fronted by six Corinthian columns.

Wyeth's attention to detail was impressive. His design specifications dictated the type and quality of materials, as well as the levels of workmanship for each component of construction. His plans called for the use of red bricks manufactured in Tennessee in the "Kingsport Hermitage Colonial" style.

Wyeth designed the interior of the mansion in the style of the great homes of the eighteenth century, with the entrance on the first floor opening to the formal entrance hall and doorways leading to the reception and dining rooms. While the original plan called for multiple guest bedrooms, considerations for cost scaled the design down to one guest bedroom and bath. The kitchen and pantry are located on the first floor, as are the family dining and living rooms, accessed by a central hall leading from the entrance hall. The second floor is reserved for the private quarters of the residents and includes four bedrooms with baths. At the basement level, Wyeth designed offices, a laundry, and rooms to accommodate heating and air conditioning systems and storage.

31

Wyeth developed several alternatives for consideration, including this version with a hipped roof.

Another alternative showed the influence of the tropical style of architecture in Florida.

The detail-oriented Wyeth lavished attention on the front doorway, a symbol of executive hospitality.

In a scene reminiscent of the first builder's sons riding the columns to the old mansion site (see pages 18-19), Wilton Carlile observed his father's installation of the cast stone columns in 1956.

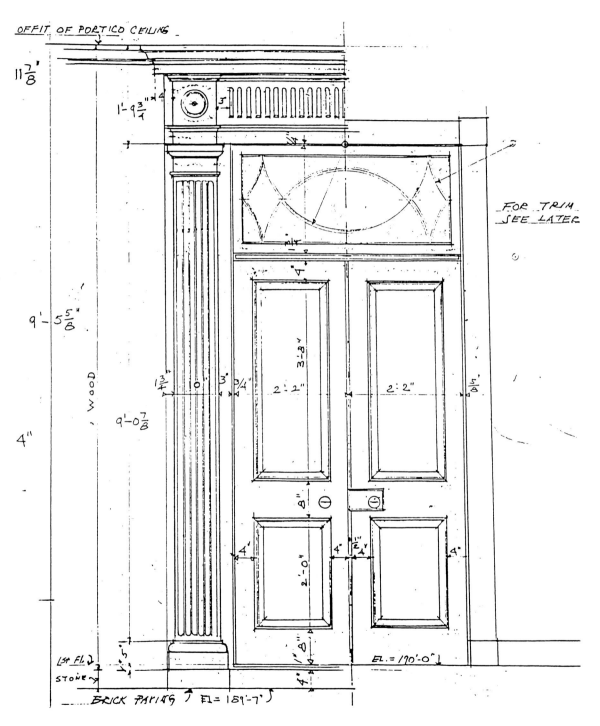

With blueprints completed, the committee awarded the building contract to Tallahassee builder J. O. Carlile, and by midsummer of 1956, his work crews had the shell of the structure in place. During construction, a copper time capsule was sealed into the wall of the entrance hall.

In a March 1957 edition of *Now in Tallahassee*, a writer expressed his anticipation for the time when the new governor's mansion would be completed and furnished: "When that day does come and when state functions begin to be held in the new mansion, Florida will have realized one of her most important dreams … a beautiful, comfortable and efficient home for the state's first citizen and his family." The furnishing of the building was entrusted to James Cogar, former curator of Colonial Williamsburg, and his work was still in the planning stage when the building was finished and opened, unfurnished, to the public in January of 1957 for the second inauguration of Governor Collins.

During the final phase of the construction, the iron fence which had surrounded the original mansion was removed. The city of Tampa volunteered its work crew and materials to install a circular brick drive and walkway at the mansion. They used salvaged brick, adding character to the newly constructed building. In 1957 after a

tour of the house, the editors of the *DeLand Sun News* expressed their opinion: "... (Florida) is a great state; and the place where its chief executive lives should reflect this fact. The new mansion for the governor is a credit to the great state of Florida."

Through two incarnations and a variety of controversies, the property at 700 North Adams Street has provided Florida's first families with a gracious place to reside, extend hospitality and conduct state business. The 1907 mansion, with the whitewashed wooden grandeur of Henry John Klutho's design, suited the excitement felt by Floridians as their state entered the twentieth century. Constructed fifty years later, the current residence embodies the dignity of Marion Sims Wyeth's plan. Designed to last three hundred years, the Florida Governor's Mansion is home to the best of Floridiana.

Four decades have attested to the genius of Wyeth's plan, the craftsmanship of Carlile's workers and the serene beauty of the Tallahassee locale.

$\mathscr{O}$PEN $\mathscr{H}$OUSE

$\mathscr{W}$elcome to the Florida Governor's Mansion. This, the home of chief executives, is that place which represents Florida's hospitality to visitors from around the nation and around the world, a home which hosts both school children and presidents.

There are treasures here, because, in one sense, the mansion is a museum — a repository for important historical collections of furniture, art and decorative objects belonging to the state. Far from being a place only for memorabilia and memories, it provides a dynamic yet comfortable backdrop for conducting state business and for extending official hospitality. It is a setting for daily events that, through the years, have become woven into the fabric of our history.

The following pages will take you to both the state rooms and those in which the resident first family conducts its private life. You will also stroll through the gardens. This is a private tour, letting you glimpse areas the public seldom sees. In these pages you may linger over an appealing piece of furniture or art, savor a spot in the garden or pause as long before the fire as you choose. No one will disturb you as you turn the pages, however slowly. Again, welcome to the Florida Governor's Mansion.

White columns gleam against warm red brick, flags
are flying and the grounds are in full spring dress.
Glimpsed through the confederate jessamine blooming
on the iron fence, the Florida Governor's Mansion
looks stately but inviting. In Greek Revival style with
Corinthian columns, the house was completed in
1957, replacing the first official residence which dated
from 1907. The central section of the house is
patterned after the Hermitage, Nashville home of
General Andrew Jackson, Florida's first territorial
governor.

Against the blue of a Florida sky, the stars and stripes and the state flag of Florida mark the entrance to the present executive mansion. A twenty-seven-star United States flag flies to one side. The twenty-seventh star was added to the blue field July 4, 1845, as Florida became a state.

A favorite pet surveys the world from among rosy springtime tulips.

Seasonal blossoms in succession fill the beds flanking the entrance walk at the front verandah, and spill from the planter boxes set between white columns. Pink, seen here, is a spring color scheme. Classically simple painted Windsor chairs on the brick floor are a hospitable touch.

This detail of one of the verandah Windsor chairs shows the graceful flaring comb-back with scrolling terminals and the horseshoe backrest.

The broad smile and gracious welcome of Jerome Cummings, mansion manager, has greeted visitors to the mansion for twenty years.

The State Rooms

The state rooms in the mansion originally were the entrance hall, the reception room, the state dining room, and the guest bedroom. A brick terrace on the northwest side of the house has since been enclosed as a Florida or garden room. In these graciously furnished and comfortable surroundings, official business and social functions take place throughout the year.

This detail of a three bowl English sterling epergne, dating from the turn of the century, shows one of a pair of charming mermen supporting the two side bowls.

The entrance hall frieze molding in Wedgwood blue adds subtle color to cream colored plaster walls. The floor of creamy Alabama marble pavers is softened by a hand-woven Persian rug. The left arm chair is an American North Shore Hepplewhite, circa 1790, in mahogany finished to look like cherry. The other is a copy of an antique chair in the Colonial Williamsburg collection of the style referred to as a "lolling chair." Brass and glass wall sconces and the central chandelier are also Williamsburg reproductions. An eighteenth century music stand holds the mansion guest book.

A mixed bouquet of early summer blossoms stands on an eighteenth century mahogany side table with carved fluting on the apron and rosette corner blocks. Above the table is a painting, *Isabelle Marie and Adrien Collumb with their Son* by John Francis Rigaud. Like most of the paintings in the state rooms, it is on loan from the John and Mable Ringling Museum of Art in Sarasota.

Governor Claude Kirk and First Lady Erika Kirk added two members to their family while residing in the mansion. A crowd welcomed newborn Erik Henry Kirk home on April 16, 1970.

Jane Collins wed John Aurell on October 1, 1960. Governor and Mrs. Collins hosted a reception for their daughter and her groom at the mansion following the ceremony.

Governor Bob Martinez and First Lady Mary Jane Martinez and their basset hound, Tampa Mascotte, greeted young visitors on Halloween.

Children seem especially fascinated with the entrance hall, where a special attraction is the ornate mirror on the wall between the windows, its opulent gilt frame carved with fruit, flowers and foliage in the rococo manner. A young visitor to the mansion once asked her hostess, "Is this the mirror the fairy princess looks in?" It reflects *The Sisters,* a painting by George Watson, on loan from the Ringling Museum.

Another favorite with visitors of almost any age, the Chippendale mahogany long case or "grandfather" clock, dates from around 1790 and bears the name of its maker, Jonathan Lees, on the dial. Brass ball finials surmount the crest, and Corinthian columns flank the elaborate face. A hand-painted moon dial, a calendar dial and a second hand are other features of this charming eight-day timepiece.

Below the Ringling painting *At the Desk* by Irving Ramsey Wiles is the porcelain *Western Bluebirds on Wild Azaleas* by Edward Marshall Boehm. A total of ninety-one four-part molds were required to cast the separate parts of this piece, which is from a limited edition of three hundred that closed in 1980.

A glimpse through the doors of the entrance hall into the state reception room.

THE RINGLING
COLLECTION

Since the second governor's mansion was completed in 1957, it has almost continuously been graced with works of art on loan from the John and Mable Ringling Museum of Art in Sarasota. The circus magnate John Ringling (1866–1936) founded the Ringling Museum to house his impressive collection of European art. Ringling left the museum to the State of Florida in his will, and after a decade of legal wrangling, Governor Millard Caldwell was finally able to gratefully accept "…the home and museum, and treasures" that Ringling wanted to give to the people of Florida.

In 1958 the governor's mansion became involved in a legal battle related to the Ringling collection. U.S. Congressman Jim Haley instituted a lawsuit against the State Board of Control challenging the museum's right to make temporary loans of Ringling paintings, which included those loaned to the governor's mansion. The narrow interpretation of Ringling's will prevailed in court until state lawmakers made explicit the museum's right to exhibit its collection

in venues other than the Ringling home in Sarasota. While the parties resolved the matter, all loaned paintings were removed from Florida's executive residence. The museum now makes temporary loans of its works to institutions across the state.

In 1980 the Florida Legislature designated the John and Mable Ringling Museum of Art as the official art museum of the state. Ringling's collection, housed in his Italianate palace on Sarasota Bay, continues to delight visitors and students.

George Watson's *The Sisters* painted in the first quarter of the nineteenth century, gracefully depicts two Scottish lassies, Georgina and Elizabeth Reay, in a pastoral setting.

The state reception room is amply scaled to accommodate large gatherings, but the furniture groupings and the furnishing's warm colors bring it down to a more intimate scale for conversation or tea by the fire. The muted colors of the large Heriz rug, dating from around 1900, anchor the room. Two Sheraton-style sofas of carved and inlaid mahogany are covered in coral damask. They stand before the black marble mantle, here dressed for a reception with flowers from the garden. *Portrait of a Young Lady* by eighteenth-century German artist Johann Georg Ziesenis hangs above the fireplace. Mahogany console tables on either side of the fireplace are neoclassical, circa 1770, and the ornate looking glasses above them are carved and gilded wood. Two open arm chairs upholstered in stripes, are reproductions of an American neoclassical design circa 1800.

A Queen Anne mahogany tea table between the settees, dating from about 1730, carries a sterling silver tea service crafted by William F. Gale & Sons of New York in 1852. ABOVE RIGHT: A closer look reveals the elaborate repoussé ornament and the exuberance of its rococo-revival design. Each domed lid has a twisted floral finial.

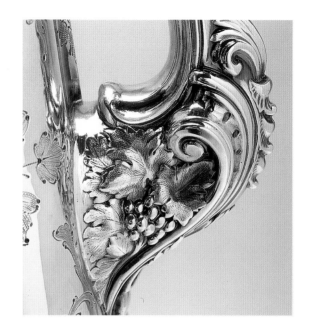

In late 1955 when the Governor's Mansion Advisory Committee began discussing plans for the interior of the new mansion, the "Williamsburg style" quickly emerged as their favorite. Such colonial revival interiors remain a classic American style, a material way to recall the founding of the United States. The committee contacted James Cogar (1907–1987) of Williamsburg, Virginia, who had led the early furnishing efforts of the Colonial Williamsburg Foundation. A native of Kentucky, Cogar was the nation's leading expert in colonial interiors, educated at the University of Kentucky, Harvard, and Yale.

Cogar met with the committee in Tallahassee, and shortly after his return to Williamsburg he wrote to Chairman Frank D. Moor: "My over all plan for the Governor's Mansion would be to have it a dignified interior, painted in a harmonious color scheme, furnished in good taste with pieces of character, and although an official residence, give it the feeling that it is a gracious home of quiet beauty that would please but not overpower those [who] were entertained there."

MANSION

INTERIOR

DESIGNER

Cogar believed he could create ". . . an interior of distinction by using as many antique pieces as may be practical" within the $80,000 budget. "Such pieces," he added, "give real atmosphere and a subtle grandeur and are doubly effective in a building which is of entirely new construction." As a matter of economy, Cogar purchased the bulk of the antique furniture in England. His assemblage of antique and high-quality reproduction pieces created a lasting style and character for Florida's Governor's Mansion.

James Cogar, shown here in his Williamsburg shop, acquired the furnishings for the mansion and directed the placement of items.

James Cogar chose to furnish the newly constructed governor's mansion with antiques of the eighteenth and early nineteenth centuries, blended with reproduction pieces for practicality as well as for economy. The mansion may project an aura of tasteful serenity from another age, but the demands of modern daily use—flexibility and convenience—are well served. Eighteenth century furniture makers used densely grained mahogany to create fluid designs, as exemplified by this chair in the state reception room. Its elegantly pierced back, tightly curled ears, and shepherd's-crook arms make for stylish seating.

Soft light and fresh flowers make a pleasant setting for music or letter writing. The handsome mahogany desk and bookcase is a circa 1770 English piece with paneled doors and candle slides. The walnut Queen Anne side chair at the desk is the oldest piece of furniture in the mansion, dating from the early 1700s.

An ebony baby grand piano offers the possibility of musical entertainment. On the wall behind it is a Ringling painting, *The Knife Grinder,* in the style of Maria M. LaFargue, an eighteenth century Dutch painter.

The lid of the humidor, shown here in detail, is centered with the state seal of Florida and a garland that includes magnolia and orange blossoms.

A small treasure, this cigar humidor from the USS *Florida,* is a part of the mansion's fabulous "battleship silver" service. From a time when the after-dinner cigar was an established ritual and the cigar industry in Florida flourished, the humidor is cedar lined to properly store its contents.

CIGAR INDUSTRY

Cigar production was a substantial segment of Florida's economy beginning in the nineteenth century. As the Cuban-American emigration of the 1860s surged into Key West, it became a vibrant cigar making center. By the 1870s, skilled workers there were producing some 62 million cigars each year. During the next decade several cigar factories were established in the Tampa Bay area, and by the turn of the century, West Tampa and Ybor City workers produced more than 111 million cigars annually. Later, with the onset of mechanized produc-

MADE
IN
FLORIDA

tion, Jacksonville and other areas became cigar producing centers. Skilled cigar makers often educated themselves while they worked by listening to a reader who was known as el lector. These dramatic readers would sit on a raised platform, la tribuna, and read to the workers

from classic novels, newspapers and tracts. The craftspeople pooled their money to pay for el lector and chose the reading selections. The Cuban revolutionary leader, José Martí, praised the educational possibilities of the lector system envisioning, "Factories that are like colleges, and … schools where the hand that folds the tobacco leaf by day, lifts the text at night." These readers held an esteemed position within the Cuban-American community. After Tampa cigar workers held a walkout in 1931, factory owners removed the readers' platforms, and radios replaced these traditional spokesmen.

In this photo from Ybor City in 1929, el lector reads the morning newspaper to cigarmakers as they work.

Cigar marketers relied on colorful printed advertising such as this box label for New Tampa Leader cigars.

For thirteen months in 1824 The Marquis de Lafayette (1757–1834), hero of the American Revolution, triumphantly toured the United States traveling to every state of the Union. Tens of thousands of Americans greeted him. Years after volunteering for the Revolutionary cause and showering the fledgling republic with his wealth, Lafayette's riches were running low. President James Monroe wrote, "His high claims on our Union are felt and the sentiment universal is that they should be met in a generous spirit." In 1824 Congress resolved to give Lafayette $200,000 and a township of land. Lafayette had befriended Richard Keith Call, the territorial delegate to Congress from Florida, and Call persuaded Lafayette to select land in Florida near the newly founded capital, Tallahassee.

President Monroe appointed Colonel John McKee, congressman from Alabama, to help select the township. McKee reached Tallahassee early in April 1825. Delayed by springtime rains, he wrote: "I have been here since the seventh but the woods are so rotten I have made but little progress in examining the country." Eventually he found the township he

THE LAND GRANT

thought to be the "…best in Florida." Territorial Governor William P. DuVal expressed to Lafayette that if he should elect to reside in the new territory, "We should receive you with open arms as our fellow citizen, our neighbor, and our friend." The aging general never visited the land America had bestowed upon him, but he gained needed capital by selling all but 300 acres.

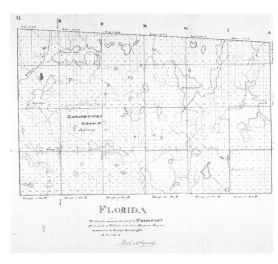

The Lafayette township, a 36-square-mile area on the northeast side of Tallahassee, encompassed valuable agricultural lands in territorial Florida.

During his Revolutionary War service, the youthful Lafayette became like an adopted son of George Washington, who was twenty-five years his senior. Depicted on horseback by Reuben Law Reed, a Massachusetts folk artist, the duo survey the battle at Yorktown.

The historic "Lafayette Clock," made in Austria in 1820, was originally a gift from the Lafayette family to the family of Robert White Williams, manager of Lafayette affairs in the Tallahassee area. The clock's round face is framed by brass and surmounted by an ormolu crest of swans, foliage and flowers. The Egyptian motifs (DETAIL, ABOVE) are typical of the period.

The Florida room, opening onto a lush garden, came into being in 1985 when a brick patio was glassed in to add relaxed and much needed space to the mansion's public areas. With its brick floor and plump upholstered seating, it is a welcoming setting for less formal gatherings such as small luncheons or suppers, or for entertaining family visitors or overflow crowds. A door is open to the garden beyond, with a view of the bronze *Manatee Dance.*

Accessories in this light and airy room — porcelain garden seats, blue and white Canton china pieces, lamp bases of hand-painted porcelain — are suited to the charming and less formal decor that provides a transition from the main state rooms to the mansion gardens. This bronze figure of a child holding a duck was sculpted by Edith Baretto Parsons and cast in bronze in 1915, the year Mrs. Parsons exhibited another similar piece at the great Panama-Pacific International Exhibition.

The table in the corner of the Florida room set for a relaxing sip of tea, has a lacy cloth centered with a glorious mix of summer flowers and greenery from the mansion gardens and greenhouse. The chairs, c. 1850, are elm and fruit wood Lancashire spindle-backs with rush seats and recall the rustic simplicity of their English country origin.

An Empire style mahogany cabinet with ormolu mountings on the east wall of the Florida room holds miniature oil portraits of Florida first ladies. Eight were painted by the late Jane Blake of Seminole, Florida; the most recent additions, portraits of Mrs. Kirk and Mrs. Mixson, were painted by Jeanne Dunne of Clearwater, Florida.

RIGHT: From upper left: Mary Holland, Mary Call Collins, Julia Bryant; Middle row: Mildred Burns, Donna Lou Askew, Erika Kirk, Adele Graham; Bottom row: Margie Mixson, Mary Jane Martinez, and Rhea Chiles.

$\mathscr{J}$OHN $\mathscr{J}$AMES $\mathscr{A}$UDUBON

As a young pioneer naturalist, John James Audubon (1785–1851) longed to explore Florida and its bird life. When, in 1831 and 1832, this most famous of America's ornithologists spent six months in the territory of Florida, the difficulties of exploration challenged his romantic perception of the wilderness, "which from childhood I have consecrated in my imagination as the garden of the United States." On foot, horseback and onboard a variety of vessels, Audubon traveled through the area in preparation for his masterful *The Birds of America.* His animated depictions of avian life captured the spirit of his subjects silhouetted against a white background. In his dramatic compositions and precise renderings, Audubon went beyond traditional conceptions of botanical illustration to create a remarkably vivid artistry.

Audubon arrived in St. Augustine in November 1831 and spent several months exploring northeast Florida. After spending a day scrambling through marshes, he wrote to his wife Lucy, "I doubt if ever a man has undergone more fatigues than I now undergo and if I do not succeed I am sure it will not be

PAINTER OF
FLORIDA'S BIRDS

for want of exertion." Assisted by a United States revenue cutter, the Marion, Audubon's crew found abundant bird life in the Florida Keys. He wrote in his journal: "The birds which we saw were almost all new to us; their lovely forms appeared to be arrayed in more brilliant apparel than I had ever before seen, and as they gambolled in happy playfulness among the bushes, or glided over the light green waters, we longed to form a more intimate acquaintance with them."

H. B. Hall's engraving of John James Audubon made shortly after Audubon visited Florida.

The *Common Gallinule,* one of several of Audubon hand-colored engravings on loan from the Ringling Museum, hangs in the Florida room. Audubon reported observing many gallinules during his Florida expedition on the St. Johns River.

A bright, quiet corner for reading has a comfortable upholstered chair and ottoman. The hand-colored Audubon print depicts the sooty tern. A bouquet of garden flowers on the table further serves to bring the outdoors inside.

Official guests at the mansion occupy the state guest bedroom. Over the years these have included several presidents of the United States, members of congress, ambassadors, foreign dignitaries such as the Duke and Duchess of Windsor, and performing artists like Pablo Casals, Helen Hays and Mikhail Baryshnikov. Twin mahogany canopy beds have turned posts above plinth legs with brass bolt covers. The cotton fabric of the canopies is printed with motifs reminiscent of eighteenth century Indian chintzes.

On the far wall are three hand-colored lithographs of nineteenth century Florida views from Francis de Castelnau's 1842 book on his North American travels. They are *Vues de la Floride, Key West Golfe du Mexique,* and *Arsenal at Key West.*

The finely done needlework seat covers that grace the Regency side chairs were crafted by Floridians. Each design is centered with a petit point medallion of Florida flowers. A late eighteenth century mahogany Pembroke table is set before a window's garden view.

LEFT: A detail of *Vues de la Floride* provides the only extant visual representation of the cascades on Tallahassee's south side, which Castelnau described admiringly: "Numerous springs exist in the neighborhood and from one of them comes a pretty stream of water that after having wound around the eastern part of the city runs into the forest and forms a charming waterfall about 16 feet high." This "beautiful rivulet", no longer in existence, helped Tallahassee become the state capital when the commissioners charged with selecting the territory's seat of government refreshed themselves near the stream.

A guest entering the state dining room knows immediately that this is an important place, a setting for significant events. It is the most dramatic of the state rooms, thanks to its spaciousness; its richness of color, surface and detail; the sparkling chandelier overhead; the gleam of silver against dark wood; and the lush, almost tropical beauty of the wallpaper that is its crowning glory.

Set for a formal dinner, the neoclassical mahogany pedestal dining table can expand to accommodate twenty-four guests. Here creamy magnolia blossoms and their glossy foliage complement the USS *Florida* silver candelabra, silver goblets, snowy linen and cobalt band china. All that remains is to usher in the guests.

In the state dining room, glimpsed through the
doorway from the entrance hall, the table is centered
with flowers. The chandelier is Louis XV style, cut glass
and brass, a piece which, according to oral tradition,
hung in a French castle when it was made about 1760.
Tiers of scrolling candle arms are suspended from a
crown and hung with faceted cut-glass garlands.
Originally it held candles, but now each arm, hung
with prisms, supports an electrified candle. Its
measurements — sixty inches from the top, not
including the chain, to the lowest pendant and thirty-
six inches in diameter at the bottom tier — give an
idea of the size and scale of the room where it hangs.

A reproduction of an 1842 design by the Zuber Company of Paris, this French scenic paper was printed with the original wood blocks, using the original technique. The design is called *Isola Bella* for an Italian island in Lake Maggiore. As shown here, it depicts flowers, foliage and birds against the blue of a cloudless sky background applied before the blocks were printed. The muted colors of green, grayed blues rose and gray, with the use of perspective and light, lend richness and interest to the walls of this large room, without overpowering its other furnishings.

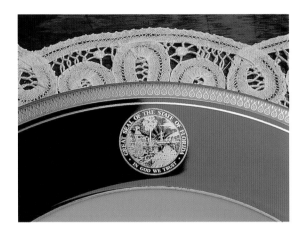

China service plates — with a cream ground and the seal of the state of Florida on a cobalt blue, gold rimmed border — were custom made.

Seen here against white lilies, this sterling silver heron candelabrum is one of a pair from the USS *Florida* silver. Great blue herons stand on three of the arms, and the shaft is patterned on a trunk of *Sabal palmetto*, Florida's state tree. The candelabra hold candles now, but originally were electrified, and had tiny fringed mica shades for each light.

USS FLORIDA SILVER SERVICE

On December 18, 1911, Floridians made tangible their pride in the new battleship named for their state during an impressive ceremony in Pensacola. Governor Albert W. Gilchrist presented to Captain Harry W. Knapp a forty-seven-piece set of sterling silver made specially for the USS *Florida.* Gilchrist spoke of the gift as emblematic of a marriage between Florida and the navy: "To us the battleship *Florida* is the greatest, largest, most powerful ship in all the world. Through the power of her guns, her machinery, her incomparable workmanship and through the intelligence and loyalty of her officers and men, the battleship *Florida* will ever carry throughout the world, the sweet, gentle suggestion of … peace."

The Florida Silver Service Commission, chaired by William A. Bours, raised $10,000 in private funds to provide the officers of the dreadnought with the elaborate hollowware.

Before its presentation to the U.S. Navy, the silver service was displayed at the Tampa Hardware Company. This broadside announced the exhibit.

U.S.S. *Florida* shown in a colorized postcard.

The engraved waiter features a likeness of the battleship along with the message: "Presented to the U.S.S. *Florida* by the People of Florida."

A silver punch cup engraved with the letter "B" was given to Bours by the members of his commission. In 1995 the cup was presented to the state by his heirs, adding the twenty-third cup to the collection.

Following the custom in the modern navy, craftsmen designed an ensemble laden with motifs of the state's cultural and natural history. The Gorham Company of New York produced the fanciful service. The pieces were chased, engraved, and also embellished with cast reliefs, such as the pelicans affixed to the twelve-gallon punch bowl. A brochure from 1911 detailing the set explained: "Florida with its tradition, its history and its wealth of natural resources, offers unlimited material to the artist in the creation of a subject which has for its theme the embodiment of the state's life." Beginning with silver forms based on the Colonial Revival, the designers sought to give "at a glance the entire story of the State for which it stands."

Elizabeth Fleming represented the state in christening the USS *Florida* on May 12, 1910. The daughter of former Governor Francis Fleming, she burst a beribboned bottle of champagne across the ship's awesome bow. As the craft slid down the ways, Miss Fleming called out, "Go, brave ship, I christen thee *Florida*." It was the third vessel to carry that name. The battleship soon set a new speed record and became the flagship of the North Atlantic Fleet. Following the United States'

entry into World War I, the *Florida* performed convoy duty ensuring the safe passage of supplies to Great Britain. In 1930, after the ratification of the London Treaty for the Limitation of Naval Armament, America, Britain and Japan agreed to reduce the number of dreadnoughts in their fleets. The U.S. Navy drew up plans to dispose of two ships, the *Florida,* and her sister ship, the *Utah.* On February 16, 1931, the *Florida* was placed out of commission at the Philadelphia Navy Yard and salvaged.

After the USS *Florida* was decommissioned in 1930, Floridians went to work to have the battleship silver returned to the state. Former first lady May Mann Jennings wrote for many when she expressed her view that "the Governor's Mansion was the proper place for the silver, where it could be used on great state occasions and be well cared for between times." Agreeing, the navy sent the exquisite silver to the mansion, where it has remained since 1931. In 1982, however, in preparation for a new nuclear-powered submarine named for Florida, the navy asked for the return of two pieces of the set. The state cabinet agreed, but the Florida Governor's Mansion Commission voted to keep the entire set at the mansion in defiance of the navy's request.

The elaborate punch bowl, the most prominent piece in the service, has a capacity of twelve gallons.

The gracefully curving border of the fruit dish features oranges, orange blossoms and jessamine.

In a playful touch, Gorham designers used alligators for the handles of the punch cups.

U.S.S. FLORIDA

In addition to the state icons, the "Centre Piece" design includes eagles' heads as symbols of federal power.

Stylized dolphins make up the feet and spout of the coffee urn.

LEFT: Governor Gilchrist said of this detail, "It will be observed that the handles of the bowl are formed in the shape of pelicans. I know of no more dignified bird than the pelican."

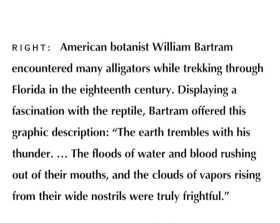

"Florida with its tradition, its history and its wealth of natural resources, offers unlimited material to the artist ..."

RIGHT: American botanist William Bartram encountered many alligators while trekking through Florida in the eighteenth century. Displaying a fascination with the reptile, Bartram offered this graphic description: "The earth trembles with his thunder. ... The floods of water and blood rushing out of their mouths, and the clouds of vapors rising from their wide nostrils were truly frightful."

Oranges and orange blossoms celebrated the state's citrus industry. A writer of a 1909 article in *The Outing Magazine* described the scent of a grove in bloom: "The volume of fragrance is utterly beyond description by the pen."

The designers sought to give "… at a glance the entire story of the State for which it stands."

Emblematic of Florida's wading birds, herons with piercing eyes and skillfully rendered feet rest on three arms of the candelabrum. John James Audubon described a group of herons which he encountered in Florida: "Their contours and movements are always graceful, if not elegant."

LEFT: The punch ladle carries a portrait of Florida Seminole Chief Osceola (probably 1804–1837). A fierce leader for native resistance, he fought for three years in the Second Seminole War before being taken prisoner under a white flag of truce. Author Thomas W. Storrow described him seven years after his death: "He was an ardent lover of his country, and as a warrior skillful beyond his opportunities. In his narrow sphere he displayed many heroic virtues; his life was engaged in a nobler cause than that which incites the actions of many whom the world calls great; and in his last moments he displayed the workings of a lofty spirit, which commands our admiration."

RIGHT: Illustrating native Floridian culture, the punchbowl is engraved with the image of Seminoles in a dugout canoe. Crafted from single trees, the long, narrow canoes were propelled by paddling and poling on Florida's abundant waterways. The circa 1900 photograph to the right shows Seminoles canoeing on the Miami River.

LEFT: This detail of Castillo de San Marcos at St. Augustine evokes a relic of Florida's colonial heritage. Begun in 1672, it is the oldest masonry building in the United States. Built of native coquina, or shellrock, the impregnable fortress saved the Spanish city from two British assaults. Sentries in the belltower kept watch over the approach to the harbor town.

RIGHT: Gorham designers placed the state seal at salient points on the service. The watercolor version on the right is from the 1920s. The 1868 legislature set the basic scheme for a seal ". . . having in the centre thereof a view of the sun's rays over a highland in the distance, a cocoa tree, a steamboat on the water, and an Indian female scattering flowers in the foreground, encircled by the words, 'Great Seal of the State of Florida: In God We Trust.'"

The Family Rooms

There must be a refuge, a haven of privacy for even the most public family — a place to relax, perhaps with close friends or other family members. Yet until the construction of the new mansion, there was no separation of state and family areas in the governor's home.

The original mansion was designed as a large private residence. The governor certainly entertained officially there, but all private homes of similar size and substance were the scene for frequent entertaining. If accounts by early visitors to Tallahassee are to be believed, the city offered virtually continuous social activity. The mansion dining room, however, seated only twelve, and kitchen facilities were what we would consider miserably inadequate. Conditions were the same in other houses, though, and the mansion staff were used to making do.

In their planning for the new mansion, the governor and cabinet set out to correct the shortcomings in the design of the old. Significantly, they stipulated that the architect should create two distinct zones, one for official state functions and one for the needs of the resident governor and family. The family areas were to have enough flexibility to adapt to the needs of the diverse first families who would make them home.

Diverse they certainly have been, with each putting its unique stamp on the pleasant suite of rooms set aside for them. Some bring a great deal of their own furniture with them, others select from state-owned pieces, including those kept in storage when not in use. It is a credit to the architect's forethought that these rooms accept change so gracefully.

The family stairwell, with its curving handrail is a tour de force by the mansion's architect Marion Sims Wyeth that visitors seldom see. Suspended in its gracefully rising arc is a glittering chandelier that adorned the original governor's mansion.

Soft morning light streams through French doors that open to the front balcony where the flags fly and where the view extends through a live oak canopy into the mansion park across Adams Street. This is one of four bedrooms on the second floor. Since this room and its bath may be closed off from the rest of the family areas, it is often used for guests who may awake early to the sound of the flags being raised.

LEFT: A breakfast tray, a book and a bowl of roses — pleasant beginnings for a busy day or an occasional leisurely morning. Soft green wallpaper, fresh white curtains and snowy pillows make a bedroom of quiet charm, one of two that overlook the front lawn. Family mementos, like the photograph on the table, happily find a place here. On the wall is an original oil painting of the Myakka River by Rhea Chiles entitled *Heartland.*

Just to the right of the family hallway one steps through the door into the state rooms. The Governor and First Lady meet here with the appropriate staff member to be briefed on the event which they are scheduled to host. The first family uses this area as a message center to assure that communication is maintained despite busy schedules.

Art is varied and eclectic in the family rooms. Above this chest are two Russian icons on loan from the Ringling Museum. Contemporary and traditional fine art blend with the treasures of the family in residence.

A setting for family relaxation — reading, games, TV — this room is also used by the first ladies for conferences with staff or with representatives of the many groups for which she serves as honorary chair. It is also an intimate retreat for after-dinner coffee following meals in the more formal rooms. It is decorated in harmony with the family dining room, glimpsed through the far doorway; together the two rooms are the nucleus for entertaining in the family area.

LEFT: The family living room has the distinction of warm Florida cypress paneling, high ceilings and crown molding. French doors open on a walkway to the front verandah, and floor length double-hung windows allow the morning sun to brighten the room. The oil painting is *The Indian Trapper* by Frederick Remington, on loan from the Ringling Museum.

Garden flowers and the curving ornament of a silver teapot are echoed in the silvery Venetian mirror. It is a pleasant vignette from a room meant for small gatherings of family and friends or a tête-à-tête discussion of the events of the day.

Breakfast for two in the family dining room includes a morning view of the south garden. The generously proportioned windows throughout the mansion are one of its most charming features, bringing indoors the shifting patterns and colors of light through every hour of the day.

In the family dining room a first lady is apt to use personal treasures of linens and tableware. The chandelier adds a note of formality, here neatly contrasted with a centerpiece of sunflowers and a charmingly informal table setting. To the left of the cabinet hangs a painting, *Florida Sunrise,* by Florida artist Christopher Still. It is a companion to one presented by the artist to President Clinton on the occasion of his visit to the mansion in 1995.

GARDENS & GROUNDS

Shown here in the green of a fresh spring morning, the governor's mansion grows ever lovelier as its gardens and landscaping mature. Within an elegant framework of spreading live oaks, plantings of shrubbery, old camellias and flowering trees soften its lines. Brick walkways pull the garden areas together, and seasonal bedding plants add color and charm.

Marking spring in beds flanking the front entrance walk, pink tulips stand in sharp relief against a white planter.

Tulips also nestle like jewels in the lush ground cover. As they fade, they are replaced by annuals grown from seed in the mansion greenhouse.

Dogwoods, native to Florida, blossom in drifts across the Tallahassee landscape like clouds of light against the sky. The mansion grounds are no exception.

Spring comes early to north Florida — so early in fact, that the Japanese magnolias may be in full bloom only to be caught by a January cold snap.

Usually, Japanese magnolias go from velvety green bud to dazzling blossom; then shattering, they display a second "bloom" of rosy petals on the ground beneath.

Ice Follies daffodils, translucent in the spring sunlight, stand knee deep in ivy across Adams Street in the mansion park.

North Florida's garden flowers, like much of its history, are tied to the Old South. Nothing could be more typical of the locale and the era than camellias, and the mansion gardens have many lovely examples. This blossom of the *Camellia japonica* variety *Grandiflora* is an elegant example.

As spring turns to summer, the curving beds that frame the south lawn will exchange their masses of bright pansies for taller, fuller annuals that bloom through the seasonal heat and into the cooler fall weather.

Fashioned to mimic the governor's mansion at avian scale, a bird house is nicely situated in a bed of impatiens and native ferns near a crape myrtle just beginning to open its frilly trusses of bloom.

If you invite them, they will come … but not always to nest where expected. This neat construction of Spanish moss and palm fiber was built in a plant on the verandah right beside the front door of the mansion.

FLORIDA'S
MARINE MAMMAL

In 1975 the legislature adopted the manatee as the "Florida state marine mammal." The Florida manatee is a subspecies of the West Indian manatee (order Sirenia). The lumbering creatures are quite large, with adults typically growing to 10 feet in length and weighing over 1,000 pounds. Able to live in both freshwater and saltwater, manatees inhabit Florida's bays, estuaries, rivers and coastal areas, where the herbivores find abundant sea grasses and other vegetation. In the winter, the sea mammals congregate near natural warm-water springs as well as near the warm-water discharge of coastal power plants. Florida manatees are an endangered species. With a low birth rate — their gestation period is at least twelve months — the human-related and natural threats to the manatee have imperiled its survival. Births occur year-round, typically of a single calf. Calves stay with their mothers for one to two years as they learn migratory routes, feeding locations and warm-water refuges. The primary human threat to manatees is collision with motorboats. In 1989 First Lady Mary Jane Martinez wrote of the sirenians: "The manatee has indeed become a symbol of our constant struggle to accommodate tremendous growth without destroying our irreplaceable wildlife heritage."

Many Floridians share a deep concern for the future of this gentle inhabitant of the state's waterways.

This 1871 engraving from *Harper's Monthly Magazine* depicts a manatee in the Florida Keys. Centuries ago, mariners believed that these sea mammals were the sirens or sea nymphs who tried, with their seductive song, to lead the ancient Greek hero Odysseus and his crew onto jagged rocks. The order to which manatees belong, Sirenia, was named for those mythical creatures.

The focal point of the side garden, or Manatee Courtyard, is this sculpture of the state marine mammal, *Manatee Dance,* cast in bronze by Tallahassee artist Hugh Nicholson. A detail above shows an appealing maternal vignette.

The pool below the manatees is filled with blossoms and foliage of Florida native plants: glistening white waterlilies, and yellow lotus, sometimes called "duck acorn" for the hard brown seeds in its pods.

Many of the plants that fill the mansion gardens are native to Florida. Their use here proves their worth for landscape planting. Florida's state tree, the cabbage palm, *Sabal palmetto,* grows naturally throughout the state.

BELOW: Other native plants pictured here include the oak leaf hydrangea, *Hydrangea quercifolia,* its white trusses turning rose as they age, its leaves creating wine-red fall color in sunny sites.

LEFT: Virginia willow, *Itea virginica,* most often occurs naturally in wet places but thrives with garden care.

Coral honeysuckle, *Lonicera sempervirens,* lacks scent but is a favorite of hummingbirds.

Beauty berry, *Callicarpa americana,* produces dainty circled flowers shown here followed by knots of magenta berries as summer wanes.

Yellow jessamine, *Gelsemium sempervirens* — not a true jasmine, but sweetly scented — ushers in spring along Florida fences and roadsides, sometimes as early as January.

Butterflies love to visit the showy milkweed, *Asclepias curasavica,* shown here backed by orange ginger blossoms atop their whorls of dark green leaves.

The butterfly bush, *Buddleia davidii* Black Knight, is a favorite nectaring plant for all species of butterflies. Annuals, such as the vinca, *Catharanthus roseus,* are added to the flower beds to "boost" summer nectar production.

In 1996 the Florida legislature named the zebra longwing the state butterfly. The zebra longwing, *Heliconius charitonius,* with its distinctive black-and-yellow stripes, inhabits woodlands and thickets throughout the length of the Florida peninsula. Gifted flyers, they are able to sail efficiently and to dart skillfully when alarmed. The longwings are regarded as among the most intelligent of butterflies; when

STATE
BUTTERFLY

An adult zebra longwing feeding on pollen from a native lantana flower.

first emerged they quickly learn the locations of flowers and communal roosts from older insects. They live slightly longer than the average butterfly with a typical lifespan of three months. Also uncommon is the longwing's ability to use pollen as a food source. Florida's environmentalists celebrated the adoption of the butterfly as a beautiful symbol of Florida's treasured natural resources.

ABOVE: Governor and Mrs. Lawton Chiles gathered with first graders in a butterfly garden at an elementary school in Tallahassee to announce the newly designated state butterfly. Capturing the symbolism of the moment, Governor Chiles said, "Like the young caterpillars, our children have the potential to soar in their spirits."

Elementary school children crafted this collage, shown in detail, of zebra longwings.

Poppies, larkspur and sunflowers are among the many garden flowers grown just for cutting. They are used in arrangements for both state and family rooms.

A bee visits a showy sunflower blossom, which may appear later in a centerpiece for a governor's "working lunch" table.

LEFT: The showy Perfume Delight is a favorite in the rose garden.

RIGHT: A pile of stacked pots waits to be used — and re-used — mute testimony to a working greenhouse and to a dedicated garden staff.

BELOW: The greenhouse makes it economically feasible to produce the vast numbers of bedding plants necessary for seasonally changing beds and planters. There is also the lagniappe of potted flowering plants — forced spring bulbs, perhaps, or dramatic orchids in bloom — to brighten the mansion rooms.

The gazebo, bricked terrace and bubbling fountain
were added to the mansion's outdoor entertaining
space during the late 1980s.

New Dawn roses, an old favorite long planted in north
Florida, cascade gracefully over the white lattice. This
reblooming rose variety displays pale pink blossoms
over a period of many months, though less prolifically
than during its first flush of bloom in spring.

Japanese honeysuckle, *Lonicera japonica,* blooms during most of the warm months. Breezes waft its traditional sweet scent throughout the gardens.

Tropical foliage plants in containers "landscape" the swimming pool, inviting in its screened enclosure.

First Families at Home

Florida's two official executive residences have been home to twenty-three of Florida's forty-one governors. Beginning with the family of Napoleon B. Broward, the first to live in a Florida Governor's Mansion, the following section presents a glimpse into the lives of those governors and their families. While serving as an appropriate setting for events of state, the two mansions have also been home to first families who have raised their children, married their daughters, seen their sons off to military service and nurtured their grandchildren as they extended the hospitality of the state to visitors.

The executive residences have changed through the years to meet the tastes and the needs of the first families. The rear of the building has been home to both a carriage house and a garage, a chicken coop and a swimming pool. World events have left their physical marks as well — during World War II a blackout room was added to the original mansion, and the cold war saw the addition of a fallout shelter. The residents of 700 North Adams Street have lived in the vortex of the tides of change. They have been, and will continue to be, principal actors in the history of the government of the State of Florida.

GOVERNOR

Napoleon Bonaparte Broward

&

FIRST LADY

Annie Douglass Broward

January 3, 1905 – January 5, 1909

In the autumn of 1907, two years from the date he was sworn into office, Napoleon Bonaparte Broward became the first governor to reside in an executive residence provided by the state of Florida. A friend who hoped for an invitation wrote excitedly: "I am so pleased that Mrs. Broward is Mistress of that New Mansion, that I just don't know how to express my appreciation to her. . . I will have my little boy, Victor to play a piece on the piano, and if his mother is feeling well, she will sing one song for the Broward family."

The Browards gathered their eight daughters on the front porch of the mansion. From left to right: Annie Dorcas, Enid Lyle, Mrs. Annie Broward holding Elizabeth Hutchinson, Elsie in the front with Agnes Caroline behind her, Florida, Governor Broward, Ellen Jeanette and Josephine.

Napoleon Bonaparte Broward was descended from a French soldier who settled in Spanish Florida after receiving a land grant from the United States for his service in the American Revolutionary War. Broward was born to Mary Dorcas Broward and Napoleon Bonaparte Broward on a plantation in Duval County in 1857. Growing up in Hamilton County in the aftermath of the Civil War, fate dealt a series of challenges to Napoleon. Orphaned by the age of twelve, he and his eight younger siblings were raised in the homes of various aunts and uncles. He acquired only a rudimentary education. His first marriage, in 1883, to Georgiana Kemp ended sadly when his young wife died giving birth to their first child. Their infant died just a few weeks later.

It was while making way on the St. Johns River as the captain of his own boat, the *Kate Spencer,* that he met his future "first lady," Annie Isabell Douglass. She traveled aboard the *Kate Spencer* on her way to Jacksonville to visit and shop, and Captain Broward fell in love with her. In the spring of 1887, when the two were married, the *Jacksonville Metropolis* reported, "The groom is one of Jacksonville's strong and manly young men. The bride is universally esteemed for graces of mind and person."

After serving with integrity as Duval County sheriff for nine years, Broward partnered with his brother Montcalm and friend George DeCottes to construct the *Three Friends,* a powerful sea-going tug rigged for offshore towing and salvaging. Reports of his seafaring escapades during the Cuban Revolution captivated Floridians. He cleverly escaped Spanish patrol boats and eluded American agents to deliver men and arms to the beleaguered coast of Cuba. Broward's bravado in the face of President Cleveland's insistence on American neutrality turned him, in the public eye, into a swashbuckling hero. He came under indictment for shipping arms to Cuba when the United States entered the war in 1898, but the case was dismissed for lack of evidence. Broward seized the opportunity presented to him by this notoriety to run for a Duval County seat in the Florida House of Representatives. He won the election at the age of forty-three.

When he decided to go after the Democratic nomination for governor, his wife, Annie, asked him how he planned to win. She recounted his reply, "I don't intend to go after the cities. ... I'm going to stump every crossroads village between Fernandina and Pensacola and talk to the farmers and the crackers and show them their top ends were meant to be used for something better than hat racks." Broward appealed directly to the special needs of Florida's rural voters, who gave him the nomination for governor and a win in the general election. As governor, Broward strove to promote Florida's economic and agricultural development. His bold program included the creation of the Board of Control, charged with coordinating the state's institutions of higher learning.

An account of Broward's inauguration in the [Jacksonville] *Florida Times-Union* speculated, "If the day is prophetic, the administration of Governor Broward will be successful for the morning dawned with clear skies and a bracing tinge in the air." Plans to build the first mansion were already under way. Until it was completed, Broward moved his wife and nine children into a rambling two-story rental house on North Monroe Street. Locals joked that there would have to be a new census taken now that the governor had moved his large family to town. After he was duly sworn, Governor and Mrs. Broward participated in the creation of the mansion with great enthusiasm. As soon as the legislature appropriated $25,000 for the project, Broward selected architect Henry John Klutho of Jacksonville to design the building. After the design was completed, Mrs. Broward selected the furnishings for the interiors.

Governor Napoleon B. Broward began his public service career as sheriff of Duval County.

In his campaign for the governor's office, Albert Gilchrist humorously countered charges of representing special interests: "No faction, machine, or ring bought him out. He will be glad to receive the support of the corporations, of the anti-corporations, the prohibitionists and the anti-prohibitionists, of the local optionists, the Christians, the Jews and the Gentiles, the Publicans and the Sinners. He would even accept support from the Pharisees."

Yours truly
Albert W. Gilchrist

On December 18, 1911, Governor Albert W. Gilchrist presented to Captain Harry W. Knapp a forty-seven-piece set of sterling silver for the USS *Florida* at the San Carlos Hotel in Pensacola.

GOVERNOR
Albert Waller Gilchrist

January 5, 1909 – January 7, 1913

Gilchrist's mother had high expectations for her three sons. She wrote to Albert: "Hunter is to be my judge, you my governor, and Rob my distinguished physician." She later became his hostess at the mansion.

Albert Waller Gilchrist was born a South Carolinian in the winter of 1858 when his mother, Rhoda Waller Gilchrist, was visiting her childhood home. His father, William Kilcrease Gilchrist, a wealthy planter in Quincy, Florida, served Gadsden County in both houses of the legislature. Young Albert distinguished himself as an honor student at the Carolina Military Institute and went on to attend the United States Military Academy at West Point. As a young man, he surveyed lands along the Gulf coast and the Charlotte Harbor area for the Henry B. Plant and Florida Southern Railway Companies.

Living most of his life in the area of Punta Gorda, Gilchrist served three terms in the Florida House of Representatives, and during his third term he was elected speaker of the house. Fulfilling his mother's earlier prophecy, he announced in 1908 that he intended to become the next governor of Florida. He won the Democratic primary and defeated both the Republican and Socialist Party nominees to win the general election.

Gilchrist was a bachelor when he took the oath of office of governor. He eschewed the mandate of the *Tallahassee Democrat* to select "a queen from the number of pretty and smart Tallahassee girls" and also chose not to live in the mansion, preferring to take up other quarters most of the year. During the legislative sessions, however, he took up residence in the mansion with his seventy-three-year-old mother, who acted as his hostess for the season's social occasions. She brought to Tallahassee the young ladies of the Gilchrist family, who were delighted to assist her with her duties at the mansion. The *Tampa Tribune* reported: "It is given by the friends of the incoming Governor that he will keep open house much after the custom that prevailed in the South when this section was in its bloom of prosperity."

Gilchrist appointed a commission, chaired by William Bours Bond of Jacksonville, to raise funds to furnish the wardroom of the newly built battleship, the USS *Florida,* with a majestic silver service, and he invited a daughter of a former governor, Elizabeth Fleming, to christen the ship when it was commissioned in 1910.

A letter to Gilchrist after a visit from a South Carolina cousin who signed herself as "Mary" hints at life at the mansion. Thanking the governor for his gift of guava jelly, she wrote, "My dear cousin — I am lonely tonight for you, the kitty and Tallahassee, and I wonder if she isn't lonesome too among the stately columns without you to pet her; for I know I should love to be enjoying the delightful breeze and chatting as we did on our last evening together."

Gilchrist stirred up a controversy in the legislature when he advocated that the birthday of Abraham Lincoln be recognized as a legal state holiday. One legislator is recorded as threatening his impeachment if such a law should pass. Among his fellow governors, though, Gilchrist had a reputation for charm. A journalist, reporting on a meeting of state chief executives in New Jersey in 1911, wrote of him: "His dry humor and southern accent, added to his fund of good stories, made his company much sought."

GOVERNOR

Park Trammell

&

FIRST LADY

Virginia Darby Trammell

January 7, 1913 – January 2, 1917

A Tampa Tribune *writer described Virginia Darby Trammell as "an unusually bright and capable woman. … The Governor's mansion will have a gracious, hospitable and thoroughly capable 'first lady of the state' in Mrs. Trammell. The social life of the state capital will be everything to be desired."*

Park Trammell was born in Alabama in 1876 to John and Ida Trammell, who moved to Polk County when Park was three years old. Young Trammell attended rural schools, worked on a farm, learned to type at the local newspaper and was educated in Florida politics at an early age as his father served as county treasurer and a state representative. In 1894, he entered the U.S. Customs Service in Tampa as a marine clerk and remained in that position during the Spanish-American War. The future governor studied law in Tennessee at Vanderbilt and Cumberland Universities, and at the age of twenty-three he returned to Lakeland to begin the practice of law. Twice elected mayor of Lakeland, Trammell went on to serve in the Polk County seat that his father had held in the Florida House of Representatives. Trammell served in the Florida Senate for four years and was president during the last two years of his term.

He ran and won his first statewide election — for the cabinet office of attorney general — when he was only thirty-two. Four years later he was elected governor of the state on the Democratic ticket. On his inauguration day in 1913, Trammell took the oath of office and promised to ". . .pledge my time, my best services and whatever ability I have, to the cause of Florida."

The age of the automobile had arrived, and although Trammell was a strong advocate for building roads, he retained for his personal use the same horse, shay, and driver that Governor Gilchrist had used.

Trammell's wife, Virginia Darby, worked shoulder to shoulder with him in his political career and was acknowledged as an effective political helpmeet. A reporter described their harmonious partnership: "Governor Trammell courts his wife assiduously as before marriage, never leaving the house for an hour without kissing her." A member of the Women's Christian Temperance Union attested of the first lady, "She is a woman who gives her time to things worthwhile and is in a position to have great influence. I believe she will use her position for the betterment of humanity." The couple became widely known for their hospitality at the mansion and entertained, among others, United States Vice-President and Mrs. Thomas Marshall.

Park Trammell works in the governor's office at the capitol. Trammell was only thirty-six when he assumed the duties of chief executive.

According to Florida historian Charlton Tebeau, Trammell championed the move to tighten election laws and provide for absentee voting, as well as the introduction of initiative referendum and recall in the law-making process. Park Trammell, elected at thirty-six years of age, remains the youngest man ever elected to the office of governor.

First Lady Virginia Darby Trammell wore this gown for her husband's inaugural festivities on January 7, 1913. A year into her residency at the mansion, journalist J. H. Reese said: "If Governor and Mrs. Park Trammell have one desirable quality that predominates over their many other admirable attributes, it is that of true hospitality."

GOVERNOR

𝒮idney 𝒥ohnston 𝒞atts

&

FIRST LADY

𝒜lice 𝒲ay 𝒞ampbell 𝒞atts

January 2, 1917 – January 4, 1921

Making use of an automobile and a loudspeaker, the enthusiastic Mr. Catts stumped the state entertaining rural audiences with his proclamation, "The Florida crackers have only three friends, God Almighty, Sears Roebuck and Sidney J. Catts!" And so it was in January of 1917 that the former lawyer and Southern Baptist minister came with his family to live in the governor's mansion .

𝒮idney Johnston Catts was born in 1863 to Samuel Catts, a wealthy Alabama planter who had served as an officer in the Confederate cavalry during the Civil War. He became a voracious reader in spite of a childhood accident which left him blinded in the left eye. He later boasted that he had read "all of the literature currently available in the libraries of the State."

The family was able to maintain their affluence through the difficult years of Reconstruction, affording the Catts children educational opportunities. The future governor attended Auburn and Howard Colleges and received a law degree from Cumberland University at the age of nineteen years. The future governor became a gifted and fiery orator as a religious conversion led him to preach in a string of Baptist pulpits in Alabama.

In 1886, Catts married school teacher Alice May Campbell. The *Tallahassee Daily Democrat* reported of their marital relationship: "Her influence has had much to do with the ambition and success of her husband." She bore eight children, six of whom survived to see their father elected to the office of governor. In 1911 the Catts family moved to Florida, where their patriarch served as minister of the First Baptist Church of DeFuniak Springs.

Catts attended a dinner for leaders of the Southern Baptist state convention held at the governor's mansion in 1912. An oral tradition holds that he took great interest in the facility and, after a complete tour, asked Governor and Mrs. Trammell how much rent they paid. When they replied that the house

The family of Governor Sidney Johnson Catts and Alice May Campbell Catts were photographed on the front porch of the mansion circa 1920.

Governor Sidney J. Catts began his career as a Baptist preacher.

was provided rent-free, his interest in becoming governor of Florida took root. In 1914 Catts continued to preach while working as a representative for a life insurance company. As he traveled the state in his Model T Ford, Catts felt he was in touch with the needs and interests of the voters. Although he had only been in the state for five years, he entered the race for governor.

The Catts campaign was extremely divisive. A court-contested battle erupted between Catts and state comptroller William Knott over the close results of the Democratic primary. Catts, convinced that the court would rule against him, took his campaign to the people, even petitioning county commission boards to place his name on the ballot as an independent. He received the endorsement of the Prohibition Party, which to that date had not been much of a force within the state. Its leaders declared that the teetotaling Catts would be their man regardless of the primary outcome. In effect, Knott became the nominee of the court while Catts became the nominee of the people. In November it was Catts by a landslide.

The new governor, true to his principles, refused to attend the inaugural ball because there would be dancing, to which he objected. He withdrew his opposition to having punch served at the ball only after officials assured him that inaugural ball punches were never "spiked." During his term, Catts actively supported prohibition and endorsed a statewide law prohibiting the manufacture, sale, or use of alcoholic beverages.

The Catts family adjusted well to life at the mansion, and it was recorded that Mrs. Catts especially enjoyed entertaining members of Tallahassee society at coffees and musicales. Alice May, the youngest daughter of the Catts, was only fourteen when she arrived at the mansion and occasionally served as chauffeur to the governor.

One month after Catts was sworn into office, the United States severed diplomatic relations with Germany, and in June of 1917 all men between the ages of twenty-one and thirty were required to register for the draft. Over 42,000 Floridians entered the service during the war, among them Florida's future governors Sholtz, Holland and Caldwell. Announcing that "the best patriot is he who raises the most grub," Governor Catts obtained permission from Tallahassee officials to keep a pigpen behind the mansion.

Catts was concerned about the welfare of the handicapped and the underprivileged. He invited the Russell Sage Foundation to evaluate Florida's social welfare programs and resources in preparation for the post-war times ahead. He also championed the passage of laws providing assistance to women with dependent children and supported the cause of women's suffrage. In 1920, Florida constitutional law prohibited a governor from succeeding himself. On December 31, Governor Catts sent a telegram to incoming Governor Cary Hardee in Live Oak: "Mansion vacated by myself and family 2:00 o'clock Sunday afternoon, January 2. We remain to extend to you and Mrs. Hardee and party welcome with hot supper prepared."

Cary Augustus Hardee

&

Maud Randall Hardee

January 4, 1921 – January 6, 1925

Hardee was an avid sportsman. Fishing, in particular, renewed his spirits. A Tallahassee publication, Smith's Weekly, *reported, "When the problems of state weigh heavily, nothing gives him greater surcease from his labors than to pack his rods and flies and hooks and hie to the woods and streams."*

Cary Augustus Hardee was born the fourth of ten children in 1876 and grew up on a farm outside of Perry in Taylor County. A newspaperman for the *Tallahassee Daily Democrat* reported on January 4, 1921: "Probably never before in the history of the state was there evidence of such a spirit of satisfaction and genuine pleasure over the inauguration of a governor as when Governor Hardee took up the duties of chief executive."

The new governor moved into the mansion with his wife, Maud Randall Hardee, whom he had wed in Madison in 1900. She enjoyed a reputation for being a gracious hostess with a special knack for planning enjoyable social events at the mansion. A Tallahassee society writer reported: "Mrs. Cary A. Hardee entertained at cards on Thursday afternoon, in compliment to her daughter, Mrs. Louise Day of Live Oak, the occasion being one of the loveliest of the social season." The writer continued by describing the mansion interior: "Opened en suite the rooms were tastefully decorated with pink duchess roses, narcissi, and other spring flowers and six tables were charmingly laid for the game of bridge, scores for the afternoon being kept on tallies in attractive designs."

As Florida's rapidly expanding population spawned six new counties, Governor Hardee exhorted the legislature to act upon the words of his inaugural speech: "We have dreamed and planned sufficiently long. Now has the time arrived for actual work and construction." Hardee labored in the lengthy process of legislative reapportionment, and he supported an amendment to the state constitution prohibiting the levying of income and inheritance taxes.

Maude Randall and Cary A. Hardee sit in generous rocking chairs on the mansion veranda with their daughter, Louise Day, and her family.

When a young prisoner was brutally killed at a private lumber camp which leased inmates of Florida penal institutions, it caused a public furor and focused national attention on the state penal system. Hardee agonized over whether or not to put a stop to convict leasing in Florida, and during this period he was plagued with bouts of depression. After conducting a thorough investigation of the prison system, the legislature passed the Prison Reform Bill, opening a new era for prisoners in state and county institutions.

❦

GOVERNOR
John Wellborn Martin

&

FIRST LADY
Lottie Wilt Pepper Martin

January 6, 1925 – January 8, 1929

An interview in Smith's Weekly *revealed that Mrs. Martin's "heart and soul are wrapped up in overseeing the affairs of the household. She will take this love for a home into the Governor's Mansion. Already she has packed her own linen and silver so it can be used immediately and both are monogrammed to lend a personal air to the spacious rooms." She also ordered flowers "to place throughout the handsome residence."*

The Martin family was well established in the citrus industry of Marion County when John Wellborn Martin was born in 1884. The Great Freeze of 1896 devastated their bountiful groves and crops and virtually destroyed them financially. Young John only attended school for four years. In 1900, at the age of sixteen, he moved to Jacksonville to work as a sales clerk for three dollars a week. Determined to better himself, he began studying law at night and gained admittance to the Florida Bar in 1914.

In 1907 Martin married Lottie Wilt Pepper of Lake City who was twenty years younger than he. After their only child died in infancy Lottie devoted herself to the success of her husband's meteoric political career. Martin practiced law in Jacksonville and, while serving three terms as mayor, earned a reputation for "common sense" governing. In 1924 he sought the Democratic nomination for governor as the "businessman's politician."

Among his opponents were former Governor Catts and Worth Trammell, brother of United States Senator Park Trammell, also a former governor. It was a heated campaign, in which Martin refuted personal charges from one of his opponents that he had paid his church tithe with a bad check. The 1924 statewide election was also the first in which the women of Florida voted, and when the final votes were tallied, Martin had a 13,000 vote majority.

Three days prior to his inauguration, John Martin, Mrs. Martin, and three of their personal household staff from Jacksonville moved into the mansion. Anticipating the duties of her new life, the first lady declared, "'I am quite sure I will have my hands full attending to my domestic duties, keeping an open house and entertaining the governor's friends and mine." Mrs. Martin became ill just before the inaugural and had to view the proceedings from her car. She rested during the mansion open house but rallied to lead the grand march at the inaugural ball.

Martin's administration came to power on the crest of an economic upturn, and he seized this good fortune to deliver on his campaign promise: "To build roads from one end of the state to the other, before the people now living are in the cemetery." His massive effort launched a spurt of growth and development, but when Florida's inflated real estate balloon burst, the economy went with it. Another blow was the devastating hurricane of 1928, when more than 2,000 residents of the shores of Lake Okeechobee died in the storm. Martin was praised for organizing assistance to the victims.

Martin's political leadership also resulted in legislation providing free text-books to Florida school children through the first six grades. Fish hatcheries and deer and quail restocking also became part of his statewide wildlife conservation program. Claude Ogilvie, a retired circuit judge and friend, said of Martin: "He had a great deal of personal charm, was a very talented speaker and a great story teller."

Members of Florida's 4-H Clubs called on Governor and Mrs. John Martin in 1925.

RIGHT: **In preparation for his inauguration, Governor John Martin gathered with his military reserve and state militia staff outside the executive residence.**

The family of John W. Martin posed on the mansion steps on the day of his inauguration on January 6, 1925. Back row, left to right: Lillian Simmons, Marshall Martin, Agnes Martin, Mrs. William Simmons, William Simmons, Melvin Tucker, Abner Withee. Front row: Alice Withee, Willie Tucker, the governor-elect, his wife Lottie Pepper Martin, Albert Owens Martin.

111

GOVERNOR
Doyle Elam Carlton
&
FIRST LADY
Nell Ray Carlton

January 8, 1929 – January 3, 1933

After the Lindbergh baby was kidnapped in 1932, Governor Carlton cautioned his three children about strangers. Little Mary told her father not to fret about her younger brother being kidnapped. She advised, "You don't have to worry about anybody getting Doyle, 'cause after they have him five minutes they'll give him back."

Florida's twenty-fifth governor was born in Wauchula, Florida in 1887 to a pioneer family who had lived in south Florida since the days when it was a territory. His great-grandfather was killed in the Seminole Wars and his grandfather was wounded in the Civil War battle at Fort Meade, Florida. The future governor came from a family of nine children born to Martha and Albert Carlton, citrus growers in what is now known as Hardee County.

Carlton was educated at Stetson University, the University of Chicago, and Columbia University, receiving a law degree from Columbia in 1912. That same year the future first lady, Nell Ray, met young Carlton while she was studying art and music at Stetson University. Their wedding took place in Tampa, where Carlton established his law practice and the couple raised their three children: Martha, Mary and Doyle, Jr.

A native of Wauchula, Governor Doyle Elam Carlton's favorite pastime was horseback riding. The *Tallahassee Daily Democrat* reported: "He is perfectly at home astride a horse, and gallops as recklessly as any cattleman at the heels of his herd."

Governor Doyle Carlton and First Lady Nell Ray posed in the mansion for this holiday greeting card photo with their children Doyle, Jr., Martha and Mary.

GOVERNOR AND MRS. CARLTON, MARTHA, MARY AND DOYLE, JR.

Carlton represented Hillsborough and Pinellas Counties in the state senate from 1917 to 1919 and later served as city attorney for Tampa. He had a reputation for being a man of simple virtues and impeccable integrity when, at the age of forty-one, he entered a hotly contested five-man race for governor. His chances seemed slim, and one pundit suggested, "that Tampa boy is good timber all right, but he can afford to wait a year or two until he gets older and more seasoned."

His tireless campaigning, combined with his gift of elocution and common sense strategies, gave him an upset victory in the primary and prompted his daughter Mary to place a hand-lettered sign on the front door of their Tampa home: "Doyle Carlton, our next Governor." In a pre-inaugural visit to the mansion, Mrs. Carlton found the home "big but not formidable." She planned to preside over the kitchen herself and to prepare her husband's favorite dishes, which included "cow peas and corn bread." The *Atlanta Journal Magazine* reported that the governor's favorite drink during the prohibition era was buttermilk.

Governor Carlton was an accomplished horseman and kept a horse and a spotted pony on the grounds of the mansion. He appreciated good music, and in the evenings the Carlton family could be heard singing in the music room to Nell Carlton's accompaniment on the piano.

When Carlton began his four-year term in 1929, Florida was reeling from the "bust" of the land boom. The economy had hit rock bottom after the stock market crash in October 1929; the state government operated at a deficit, banks failed and jobless rates soared. Carlton gained control of the banking industry to protect consumers and made painful but necessary cuts in the state payroll, beginning with a cutback of his own annual salary from $9,000 to $7,500. At the same time, Florida's citrus groves were plagued by the devastating effects of the Mediterranean fruit fly. The governor met with President Hoover, who directed federal dollars toward financial relief for the growers. Carlton vetoed a pari-mutuel bill to legalize gambling at horse and dog tracks in spite of a proffered bribe of $100,000 and threats of bodily harm. The governor was reported to be guided by the adage "the approval of tomorrow is far better than the applause of today." The legislature, however, overrode his veto.

The Great Depression brought a change of life style at the executive residence. The family entertained state guests at their own expense and provided food for hungry hoboes who knocked on the back door of the mansion. Carlton's sense of compassion tempered his fiscal conservatism, and he once exclaimed, "God help this state if it is too chintzy to do its part to help its own hungry, needy people."

GOVERNOR

David Sholtz

&

FIRST LADY

Alice Mae Agee Sholtz

January 3, 1933 – January 5, 1937

The Sholtz's youngest daughter, Lois, remembers how her mother took all the fish out of the mansion fish pond and put them in buckets in the basement so that her daughters could learn to swim in the pond. Lois recalls being so concerned that the poor fish would die at her expense that she repeatedly stole into the basement to make sure they were alive. Sure enough, all the fish went back into the pond unscathed after the children had completed their lessons.

David Sholtz's parents, Anne and Michael emigrated from Germany to Brooklyn, New York, where David was born in 1891. Michael Sholtz was a successful businessman who invested heavily in building projects in Daytona Beach.

David attended public schools in Brooklyn and went on to study at Yale University. He received his law degree in 1915 from Stetson University in DeLand, Florida, and chose to practice law in Daytona Beach. The next year, he made a successful bid to represent Volusia County in the Florida Legislature but resigned the office to enlist in the navy during World War I. In 1925, Sholtz married the former Alice Mae Agee of Norfolk, Virginia, and the couple raised three children, son Michael and daughters Carolyn and Lois.

Sholtz served as president of both the local and statewide chambers of commerce. In 1932, he joined seven candidates in a race for the Democratic nomination for governor. Some cynics put his odds of success at 200 to 1. Full of an infectious self-confidence, Sholtz used a flat-bed truck mounted with a public address system to amplify his persuasive oratory. To the surprise of many, he ran second to former governor John Martin and went on to upset him in the run-off. On January 3, 1933, Sholtz became the twenty-sixth governor of the state of Florida.

The *Tallahassee Daily Democrat* reported of the new first lady: "Mrs. Sholtz brings with her to Tallahassee an experience in child welfare and civic work as well as the social charm which has endeared her to many friends in Daytona Beach." Thousands responded to an invitation to a mansion open house on the afternoon of the inauguration. The Tallahassee paper gave details of the outstanding celebration: "Red roses were used in the reception, drawing and music rooms and hall, while japonica, narcissi and other cut flowers were very lovely in the study and throughout the upstairs."

When the family moved to the mansion, the three Sholtz children ranged in age from three to five years old, and for the first time a lock was put on the front gate. The family spent summers in North Carolina, but because of the austere economic conditions of the depression, they did little state entertaining. When the couple did entertain, the little girls would quietly sit in their nightgowns at the top of the stairs and peer out through the railing, marveling at the elegant dresses worn by the visiting ladies.

Sholtz was labeled the "New Deal Governor" because of a close relationship with President Franklin Roosevelt that began in 1933 when Giuseppe Zangara, a crazed anarchist, made an attempt to assassinate Roosevelt in Miami. The assassin missed the President, but his bullets fatally wounded

With gubernatorial ambitions, David Sholtz and Alice Mae Sholtz gathered for this photo with their children Michael and Lois in their hometown of Daytona Beach.

Governor David Sholtz became known as the "New Deal governor" for his close ties with President Franklin D. Roosevelt and his program to fight the Great Depression.

Chicago mayor Anton Cermak. Sholtz was there to officially greet the President and, seeking to comfort F.D.R., accompanied him in his Pullman car as far as North Carolina. As a result of that friendship, federal funds began to flow into the state's impoverished coffers. Sholtz managed to balance the state's budget as well as provide free textbooks for all public schoolchildren. He established the Citrus Commission and the Florida Park Service. A state beverage department also grew out of the repeal of the prohibition amendment, and a liquor tax was an important new source of revenue. While the state did not fully recover from its economic morass, Sholtz was responsible for improved long-range fiscal planning and for securing millions of dollars in federal funding for Florida.

Born in 1871, Fred Cone was the ninth of thirteen children in a family whose ancestry dated back to Florida's territorial days in Columbia County. He attended public school in his home county and later attended Florida Agricultural College and Jasper Normal College. His friends called him "Old Suwanee" for the river that flowed by his boyhood home in the piney woods of north central Florida, and for the backwoods mannerisms he adopted.

For a short while, Cone taught public school in north Florida. Then, after his admission to the Florida Bar in 1892, he moved to Lake City where he practiced law and became a banker. He served three terms as mayor of Lake City and was elected to the Florida Senate in 1907. Recognized as a leader by his peers, Cone was elected to serve as senate president.

GOVERNOR

Frederick Preston Cone

&

FIRST LADY

Mildred Victoria Thompson Cone

January 5, 1937 – January 7, 1941

During the 1936 campaign, Cone berated Governor Sholtz for the lock he had placed on the front gate of the mansion. With backwoods vernacular which belied his learning, Cone pledged to "fling open them gates so the people can visit their mansion anytime they want to." He carried out his pledge on the eve of his inauguration when he opened the house to newspaper men for an informal conference.

Nicknamed "Old Suwanee," Frederick P. Cone was sixty-five when he took the oath of office, the oldest of Florida's governors to date.

For the inaugural festivities of 1937, First Lady Mildred Victoria Thompson Cone wore an ivory gown of chantilly lace.

Cone married twice. His first wife, Ruby Scarborough of Lake City, died in 1923, leaving him with his only child, Jessie Francis. In 1929, he married Mildred Thompson of Macclenny. Eloise Cozens of the *Florida Times-Union* wrote that Mrs. Cone's friends described her as a "lady who remained a lady — first, last and always, and who maintained the same sweet disposition, in the Mansion, out of it, everywhere."

As the Great Depression weighed heavily on Floridians, many were attracted to the conservative approach to government advocated by Fred Cone in his campaign for governor. According to historians, he was no "New Dealer," but he promised to "Clean the budget to the bone, then scrape the bone." In 1937, at the age of sixty-five years, he became the oldest Floridian in this century to be inaugurated governor.

The press apparently enjoyed Cone's downhome manner. Herbert Bayer of the *Florida Times-Union* reported that some ladies of Tallahassee had spent the day in the mansion decorating for the inaugural reception, about which the governor-elect said, "'I'll have to have supper in the kitchen because I know the rooms have been so fixed up that we can't get into them.'" He also announced the attire he was planning to wear the next day: "'I'll have to 'put on the dog' as they call it back home.'"

The festivities at the inaugural open house were marred when the governor's sister, Mrs. Jessie Wadsin, slipped on a rug and fractured her hip. This unfortunate event was the first of a series of medical problems that beset the Cones. When Governor Cone suffered a double coronary occlusion during his second year in office, the downstairs music room was converted into a bedroom for his extended recuperation. The courts rejected a petition to declare him physically unfit to serve, and he continued to run his office from the mansion, relying heavily on his long-time secretary Ella Neill of Lake City and other staff members.

As governor, Cone's program advocated lower taxes and a reduced government budget. He supported the licensing of motor vehicle drivers and using the licensing fees to fund the Highway Patrol. The Murphy Act provided for the sale of tax-delinquent property, a legacy of Florida's pre-depression real estate boom, to put property back on the tax rolls. The governor also fostered the development of Florida's widely praised exhibit at the 1939 World's Fair.

GOVERNOR

Spessard Lindsey Holland

&

FIRST LADY

Mary Groover Holland

January 7, 1941 – January 2, 1945

"Governor Holland's hobby is Florida. Nothing else."
—*Maybelle Manning,* Miami Daily News, *1941*

In 1940 Floridians elected their twenty-eighth governor, Spessard Lindsey Holland. He was born in Bartow in 1892, the eldest of three children born to Benjamin and Virginia Holland. His father was a citrus grower and his mother a teacher. Holland attended public school and went on to graduate from Emory University in Atlanta where he excelled academically and played on the baseball, basketball and football teams. He graduated from the University of Florida Law School in 1916, and although he had

qualified as a Rhodes Scholar, he voluntarily joined the armed forces when the United States entered World War I. He saw action as a gunner and observer with the 24th Flying Squadron in France and was one of only eighteen men to be decorated with the Distinguished Service Cross for valor. Mustering out at the rank of captain, young Holland returned home to Bartow and wed his sweetheart, Mary Alice Groover, a native of Ft. White, Florida. After serving for eight years as county judge, he went into the private practice of law in 1928 and represented his home county in the state senate from 1932 to 1940.

The 1940 governor's race found Holland and ten other men, including Fuller Warren — who would later be elected to the office — vying for the nomination for governor on the Democratic ticket. Holland won a primary run-off by 72,000 votes, and with the Republicans offering no opponent, he received 334,152 votes in the general election.

In 1941 the Hollands, with their four children, moved from Bartow to the governor's mansion for the restrained World War II era inaugural. Their oldest son, Spessard Lindsey, Jr., was attending Emory University at the time. Sixteen-year-old Mary Groover unpacked her sewing machine with which she proudly fashioned her own dresses. Eleven-year-old Billie Ben enjoyed his BB gun and became renowned for the bantam chickens he raised on the mansion grounds. Daughter Ivanhoe, aged seven, would become known as a Tallahassee beauty. The governor was a music lover and would often announce his arrival home for lunch by playing a piano medley in the music room.

Mrs. Holland was engaged in a variety of civic projects in addition to running the household. She led a campaign for clean and well-supplied rest rooms along Florida's highways, enlisting the support of "all the women in Florida, because when women really get started on a project, they can do more than the state's militia." As a pastime, she kept a collection of seashells. The pride of the house was said to be the den, where Governor Holland housed his massive collection of books on Florida.

When the Hollands moved into the house, it was thirty years old and needed repairs. The governor, writing a friend who had recently visited the mansion, compared it to a Methodist parsonage. "Yes, we are busy trying to fix up the Mansion," Holland wrote, "They just treated us for termites this morning and we could hardly get in for lunch. ... I think the fine old house is going to be greatly improved as a place to be lived in by reason of the changes." Late in 1941 the Hollands added a projector and screen to the playroom on the third floor, where, as the governor wrote, "Billie Ben has already learned to be quite a proficient operator." When the Hollands' residency ended, the outgoing Mrs. Holland gave the new first lady, Rebecca Caldwell, a friendly hug and said, "You'll love it here in the mansion. I know you'll be happy."

The overriding concern of the Holland administration was the coordination of state and federal resources in the war effort. The governor was an avid sportsman and naturalist, and he established the Florida Game and Fresh Water Fish Commission, as well as giving leadership for the creation of the Everglades National Park. He also supported efforts to build better highways through gasoline taxes, and he increased assistance to blind and elderly Floridians.

The Holland family bundled up for the inauguration downtown. Left to right: Mary Groover, Spessard, Jr., Mrs. Holland, Ivanhoe, Governor-elect Spessard Holland, Billy Ben, with their dog Mike.

GOVERNOR
Millard Fillmore Caldwell
&
FIRST LADY
Rebecca Harwood Caldwell

January 2, 1945 – January 4, 1949

Having teenagers in the house added a bit of spice to Mrs. Caldwell's role. She recalled a time that their two daughters were entertaining twenty classmates from Leon High School when the governor called to tell her that in ten minutes the Supreme Court justices and their wives would be arriving at the mansion for dinner. Mrs. Caldwell managed the arrangements for both groups by serving the young people while the dignitaries visited.

Millard Caldwell was born in 1897 near Knoxville, Tennessee. His father practiced law, farmed, and managed the family's extensive land holdings. Caldwell attended Carson Newman College in Tennessee, served as an army lieutenant during the First World War and studied law at the University of Virginia. Prior to her marriage to Caldwell on Valentine's Day in 1925, Rebecca Harwood was the first woman superintendent of a Virginia county school board. The couple moved to Milton, Florida, where Caldwell became active in politics. He served as city attorney and went on to represent Santa Rosa County in the state legislature. In 1932, he logged 14,800 miles in sixty days, crisscrossing his congressional district in a Model A Ford as he campaigned for a seat in the United States Congress. He won and served from 1933 to 1941. As a member of the Congressional Foreign Affairs Committee, he represented the United States at interparliamentary conferences at the Hague and Oslo.

Tragedy struck the Caldwell family when their only son was killed by a hit-and-run driver while they were living in Washington, D.C. The Caldwells and their two daughters, Sally and Susan, returned to Florida to live on Harwood Plantation, a rambling estate northwest of Tallahassee. In 1944, friends urged Caldwell to seek the Democratic nomination for governor. He ran and defeated six candidates in two primaries.

When a *Tampa Tribune* reporter asked Mrs. Caldwell about her plans for life in the mansion, she responded, "I am going to try to run it according to the best tradition of the Old South. I want the mansion to be a home, and I want the public to take pride and an interest in it." The governor's daughters remember pajama parties, jukebox music, ping pong tournaments and dances in the upstairs of the mansion as great fun during their teenage years. Governor Caldwell forbade his daughters to date, but Susan remembers the one special occasion when her husband, then a teenage boy, nervously walked into the mansion library to introduce himself to the governor and ask his permission to take Susan out for a soda.

The *Tallahassee Daily Democrat* reported an incident in which several local women were at the mansion arranging flowers and decorating for a large gathering scheduled for that evening. Flowers and greenery in large bunches were scattered throughout the ground floor: "Mrs. Caldwell was coming down the stairs when the doorbell rang and Martin Tanner, the butler, announced the Duke and Duchess of Windsor. Even amidst all the resulting confusion, the three enjoyed themselves."

Governor Caldwell preferred to conduct state business in his office at the capitol. He later remembered: "I don't think in the four years I was in the

Governor Millard Caldwell, shown here in July of 1947, later served on the Florida Supreme Court.

Budding hostesses Susan and Sally Caldwell served punch from the USS *Florida* punchbowl.

mansion I had ten calls at night about business. … I let it be understood that I would not handle it in the mansion and that I would not have meetings or conferences in the mansion." While in office he advocated the mansion be moved to a spacious twenty-acre hilltop outside of town. In 1953, when the siting of the new mansion was being determined, he wrote a letter to then State Senator LeRoy Collins describing the Adams Street block as "impossibly small." He went on: "With good right the people of Florida contemplate a mansion so located and designed as to reflect dignity and credit upon the State. If the old site is used, the one question to be asked over the next hundred years will be 'Why was it ever put in that place?'."

Governor Caldwell expanded state services to meet Florida's postwar population boom. He opposed the "Porkchop Gang," comprised of north Florida lawmakers, in a fight for greater equality of legislative representation. His efforts resulted in a significant reapportionment of state senate districts in the Florida panhandle. Additionally, the Minimum Foundation Program, ensuring basic academic standards for public school students, was enacted during his administration.

GOVERNOR

Fuller Warren

&

FIRST LADY

Barbara Manning Warren

January 4, 1949–January 6, 1953

Warren's gift for oratory became evident at an early age; by age ten he was called on to entertain hometown groups. During his years at the University of Florida, he was sophomore class president, cheerleader, newspaper reporter and member of the university's middleweight boxing team.

Florida's thirtieth governor was born in Blountstown in 1905, the third of seven children. His father was a lawyer and his mother a teacher. At the age of twenty-one, while still a university student, he was elected by the people of Calhoun County to the Florida House of Representatives. After graduating from Cumberland Law School in Tennessee, Warren began the practice of law in Jacksonville in 1929. His early political career also included three terms on the city council. At the age of thirty-five, he made an unsuccessful but surprisingly effective bid in the 1940 gubernatorial race.

During World War II Warren was commissioned as a naval gunnery officer and made twenty crossings of the Atlantic Ocean aboard merchant ships. He wrote three books on speechmaking, as well as a widely read weekly newspaper column that increased his statewide recognition. In 1948 he

A gifted orator, Fuller Warren made hundreds of speeches during his 1948 "All Florida Campaign" for governor. Earlier he had written three books on public speaking, including *Eruptions of Eloquence* in 1932.

captured the Democratic nomination for governor in a primary run-off, defeating his Republican opponent in the general election.

The [Tallahassee] *Sunday News Democrat* reported, "The mansion, recently renovated, stands in readiness for its new occupants." Warren asked his younger sister Alma to serve as first lady, as he was divorced at the time of his election. She took up her duties with confidence and enthusiasm. Shirley DeGinther, a staff writer for the *Tallahassee Democrat,* wrote of her: "Reflecting southern hospitality, an important attribute for Florida's first lady, Miss Warren takes a genuine interest in everyone she meets."

Faced with entertaining numerous guests on a meager $100-a-month food budget, Alma Warren became a creative economizer. She and butler Martin

Tanner served vegetables from the garden they tended on the mansion grounds. She also took pride in raising some fifty New Hampshire Red chicks which were housed in a coop at the rear of the building. Floridians also sent gifts of food. She related to the *Tampa Daily Times,* "We are like a Methodist preacher when it comes to getting foodstuffs for gifts. … We won't turn any of it down and we are most grateful for the thoughtfulness of our friends." Although her brother preferred steak, she described their typical menu as "an ordinary Florida cracker meal."

Six months after he took office, Warren married a Californian, twenty-three-year-old Barbara Jean Manning. In a story which attracted national attention, Frank Neill, reporter for the *Miami Herald,* wrote, "She has a whistle-stop figure and a mind to match. The teen-age set probably would

Alma Warren helped adjust her brother's tie in preparation for his inauguration in January of 1949.

Newly married Barbara Warren is pictured in front of blooming azaleas on the south side of the mansion.

tout her as a slick chick." Barbara Warren had quietly attended the inauguration festivities the previous January and was introduced to the southern custom of eating black-eyed peas and hog jowls on New Year's Day. She required some instruction on the pronunciation of the word "jowls." Although no longer filling the role of first lady, Alma stayed on at the mansion to help her new sister-in-law manage the household.

As governor, Warren sponsored legislation that required the fencing of cattle land to keep cows off the highways. He banned the Ku Klux Klan from public places, calling them "covered cowards, hooded hoodlums and sheeted jerks." He revised citrus codes to improve the standards of this important agricultural industry and also instituted reforestation and fire protection programs to restore Florida's depleted forestry resources. Warren was stymied by an empty treasury and failed in an attempt to raise revenues. Instead, he turned his energies toward promoting Florida's tourism and industry, which produced a significant boost to the economy.

GOVERNOR

Daniel Thomas McCarty

&

FIRST LADY

Olie Brown McCarty

January 6, 1953 – September 28, 1953

The McCartys' daughter, Frances Lela, was used to seeing her dad in "work clothes" suitable for farm work. Seeing him in a white shirt and tie, she asked, "Where are you going, Daddy?" After the governor explained that he was going to work, she said, "You aren't going to wear those clothes to work are you?"

Mrs. McCarty is pictured on the south lawn of the mansion with two of her three children, Frances and Michael.

Dan McCarty was the first governor to hail from the southeast section of the state. He was born in 1912 in the coastal town of Ft. Pierce and was the eldest of the four children of Daniel and Frances McCarty. The McCarty family had moved to the Ft. Pierce area in 1896, where his father engaged in citrus and pineapple growing and ultimately owned extensive agricultural land in St. Lucie County. The future governor attended public schools and received a degree from the College of Agriculture at the University of Florida, where he was active in sports. When he returned to St. Lucie County, he organized a cooperative of growers called the Indian River Citrus Association.

It was 1937 when McCarty was elected to represent St. Lucie County in the Florida House of Representatives. His peers unanimously elected him

Olie Brown McCarty and Daniel Thomas McCarty, with the traditional top hat, prepare for his inauguration on January 6, 1953.

speaker of that body at the age of twenty-nine, the youngest member ever to serve in that capacity. The editors of the *Tampa Tribune* praised their decision, calling McCarty a "'little county' man with a knowledge of 'big county' problems."

He courted Olie Brown, a colleague in the Indian River Citrus Association, and married her before leaving to serve in the army during World War II. During his military service he rose to the rank of colonel. His many decorations for meritorious service in combat in Africa and at "D-Day" in France included the Purple Heart. After returning to civilian life, he made an unsuccessful bid for the Democratic nomination for governor in 1948, but four years later he defeated five candidates to win the office.

The McCarty clan — Dan and Olie, Frances Lela, Lola, Danny and their Boston terrier, Tarheel — drove to Tallahassee from Ft. Pierce in January of 1953 in their light blue, wood-paneled station wagon. Pat Pinkerton, writing for the *Tallahassee Democrat,* explained that although the mansion was fully equipped, the McCartys had brought quite a few belongings with them: "Mrs. McCarty said that the youngsters' toys, beds and other items such as linens, silver, clothing, several table lamps and her husband's hunting and fishing equipment constituted a fair sized packing job." A gracious and capable woman, Olie McCarty had proved her mettle by running the family citrus business while her husband was serving in the army overseas.

In the second month of his four-year term, tragedy struck the forty-one-year-old governor and his family. On February twenty-fifth, after a busy day at the mansion, he suffered a heart attack from which he never fully recovered. Through the following spring and summer he performed most of his work from the executive residence and, when able, made weekly visits to his office.

In his first public appearance after the attack, he rode in a parade. Shortly after this outing, a bout with pneumonia proved fatal. He died on September 18, 1953, in Tallahassee Memorial Hospital. Florida Supreme Court Chief Justice B. K. Roberts eulogized, "the untimely death of Governor Dan McCarty is a tragic loss to the whole state." Commissioner of Agriculture Nathan Mayo said, "I think he had the makings of going down in history as one of our greatest Governors."

GOVERNOR

Charley Eugene Johns

&

FIRST LADY

Thelma Brinson Johns

September 28, 1953 – January 4, 1955

The family was vacationing at their summer camp on Crystal Lake when Johns learned of McCarty's death. He proceeded to Tallahassee and visited the family of the late governor before Supreme Court Justice John E. Mathews swore him into his new office. After taking the oath he lamented ,"This is a very sad and solemn occasion."

Florida's constitution did not provide for a lieutenant governor at the time of Dan McCarty's death. Until an election could be held, the title of governor passed to the president of the senate, a position held by Charley Johns, who served as acting governor for fifteen months after McCarty's untimely death.

Johns was born in Starke in 1905, the son of Everett and Annie Johns. His older brother, Markley, had been elected president-designate of the Florida Senate in 1933, but died before he could assume office. This loss left Johns with a burning ambition to become senate president. He attended the University of Florida but ran out of money before he could complete the requirements for a degree. He became a conductor with the Seaboard Airline Railway, became successful in the insurance business and founded

the Community State Bank in Starke. He married Thelma Brinson, also a native of Starke, and they raised two children, Charley and Markleyann. Johns was elected and served one term in the Florida State House of Representatives in 1935. Two years later he was elected to the Florida Senate, where he served for twenty-nine years.

After the McCarty family left Tallahassee, Governor and Mrs. Johns and their family took up residence in the mansion. Thelma Johns remembered life in the mansion as a ". . .rich and rewarding experience." During their tenure, she remarked to a *Florida Times-Union* writer that being governor had not changed her husband's manner. Mrs. Johns said, "'He hasn't changed a bit. He still brings guests home to dinner at a moment's notice, still can't find the right shirt without help, and still spoils our young daughter Markleyann.'" Their daughter, a sixth-grader when she moved to the

Governor and Mrs. Charley Johns prepare to welcome guests prior to a Christmas party in 1953 with their daughter Markleyann.

residence, played table tennis on the third floor with neighborhood friends and practiced her piano skills in the music room.

While serving as acting governor, Johns lent support to the rapid construction of highways throughout Florida and clamped down on illegal gambling. In 1954 he lost the campaign to complete Governor McCarty's unexpired term to LeRoy Collins, but Johns retained his seat and seniority in the Florida Senate, representing Bradford and Union counties.

GOVERNOR

Thomas LeRoy Collins

&

FIRST LADY

Mary Call Darby Collins

January 4, 1955 – January 3, 1961

Mrs. Collins shared her hopes for the new mansion to a United Press *reporter: "'It belongs to every citizen in Florida. I hope everyone working on it, even if he's just laying cement, will take real personal pride in the job and create something the whole state can be proud of.'" She continued, "'I'll admit I've lost a lot of sleep over it. I wake up at night worrying because it's not like building our own home. Here you've got a lot of people to please.'"*

Florida's thirty-third governor was a native Tallahasseean, born in 1909. LeRoy Collins was one of six children of Marvin Collins, a grocer, and the former Mattie Brandon. He attended public school in Leon County and went on to the Eastman School of Business in Poughkeepsie, New York. He studied law at Cumberland University in Tennessee and was admitted to the Florida Bar in 1931, choosing his hometown for his practice. In 1932 he married Mary Call Darby, a great-granddaughter of two-time Territorial Governor Richard Keith Call.

By 1934 Collins was representing Leon County in the state house of representatives, a post he held until he was elected to the state senate in 1940. He resigned his seat to enter the U.S. Navy in the Second World War. When he returned home, he was re-elected to the senate in 1946 and again in 1950. Collins won the Democratic primary to serve out the remaining two years of Dan McCarty's term of office. When he ran for re-election and won, he became the first Florida governor to serve two consecutive terms.

Governor and Mrs. Collins moved into the mansion in 1955 with their four children: LeRoy, Jr., a nineteen-year-old attending the U.S. Naval Academy; Jane, a sixteen-year-old student at Leon High School; Mary Call, twelve years old and in junior high; and four-year-old Darby.

As the site of the first mansion was being cleared, the Collinses moved to the Grove, a stately old mansion located next door to the executive residence, which served as the interim governor's mansion while work progressed on the new building. In the spring of 1957, Governor Collins and his family moved into Florida's new governor's mansion. They resided in the new mansion for almost four years, setting a genteel precedent for future first families.

While serving as governor, Collins sought to broaden the state's economic base. He minimized racial strife in the state during the national civil rights movement. He established the community college system and continued a career-long advocacy of excellence in the educational system of Florida. After serving as chairman of the Southern Governor's Conference in 1960, he became the first governor since the Civil War to serve as permanent chairman for the Democratic National Convention. Through the State Development Commission he sought to provide a strong basic economy for the state based on industry, agriculture and tourism. He also led progressive reforms for the state's students from grade school to college age.

GOVERNOR

Cecil Farris Bryant

&

FIRST LADY

Julia Burnett Bryant

January 3, 1961 – January 5, 1965

Bryant spent his freshman year of college at Emory University in Atlanta. He apparently had some reservations about the experience. The next year when his parents put him on board a train in Ocala to return to school in Georgia, he decided to get off at Gainesville and attend the University of Florida.

This 1960 photograph shows Governor LeRoy Collins in the cypress-paneled executive office on the ground floor of the mansion.

The Collins family gathered in the state reception room for this picture in 1960. From left to right, beginning with the front row: Jane, Darby, Mary Call, Governor and Mrs. Collins, daughter-in-law Jane and LeRoy, Jr.

Farris Bryant was born in 1914 on the family's farm outside of Ocala, one of three children born to Cecil and Lela Farris Bryant. His father was an early member of the State Board of Accountancy. His uncle, Ion Farris, twice served as speaker of the Florida House of Representatives, providing a role model for the future state leader. Bryant attended public school in Marion County and received a business degree from the University of Florida in 1935. He went on to graduate from Harvard University Law School.

With his law degree in hand, Bryant moved to Tallahassee to work for the state comptroller. Julia Burnett, a native of Madison, Florida, graduated from Florida State College for Women in 1939. Bryant met her while she was playing tennis, and within a week they were engaged to be married.

126

After a New York City honeymoon, the newlyweds moved to Ocala where he entered private law practice.

Marion County voters gave Bryant his first elective post as state representative in 1942, but he resigned his seat to enlist with the navy during World War II. He attained the rank of lieutenant and was assigned antisubmarine and gunnery duties in the Atlantic and Pacific Oceans. After the war he returned to Ocala and in 1946 was again elected to the state house of representatives, where he served for ten years. He became speaker of the 1953 session.

In what he later remembered as a "warm-up" contest, he lost the 1954 Democratic primary race for governor to LeRoy Collins. Four years later he engaged in a fierce primary fight with a past resident of the governor's mansion, Doyle Carlton, Jr. He was elected Florida's thirty-fourth governor as the candidate for the Democratic Party.

Farris Bryant, pausing on the mansion grounds, later reflected on the office he held four years: "As governor, one is not the master of his own life. The demands are so many and so insistent that you can spend your term just meeting other people's demands."

The Bryants and their three daughters were the second family to take up residence in the new executive mansion. Soon after moving in, First Lady Julia Bryant explained: "'Now we must rearrange our thinking, our goals and our lives to meet the challenges of our new way of life … the children are prepared for a gold-fish bowl existence for the next four years.'" Writing for the *All Florida Magazine*, Hettie Cobb commented on the energy Mrs. Bryant infused into the operation of the house: "She organizes with the finesse of an industrial engineer and delegates authority like a trained executive." Mrs. Bryant said the staff at the mansion allowed "'. . . more time for me to taxi the children to school, to music and so forth — and to do many other things that might otherwise go undone.'"

The Bryants brought their piano with them when they moved from Ocala, supplementing the mansion's existing piano so that both daughters could practice at the same time. They were Cecilia, a ninth-grader named for her father, and ten-year-old Adair, whom her mother described as "a tomboyish pixie who loves to tease." The eldest daughter, Julia, attended nearby Florida State University. She lived in a campus dormitory but visited her family at the mansion on weekends.

The family missed their swimming pool in Ocala and welcomed the offer of the Florida Swimming Pool Industries Association to construct a pool on the grounds of the mansion. During their term the aging garage was removed and a more modern one constructed, as well as a dressing and cabana area for the pool. With the advent of the Cuban missile crisis, the Governor's Mansion Commission approved plans in 1961 to construct a nuclear fallout shelter on the grounds. Commission chairman Warren Sanchez told the *Florida Times-Union:* "'We feel it makes good sense to have a designated area from which the Governor and his assistants can direct the vital affairs of our state in time of emergency. The available space at the residence provides a well-suited location for this purpose.'"

After a number of occasions when unannounced groups stopped by the mansion expecting a guided tour, Julia Bryant instituted a new visiting policy: "at homes" at the mansion on Thursday afternoons, when she offered guests hospitality and tea. These visitors could park in the newly completed parking area across from the mansion. Writing for his syndicated column *Cracker Politics,* Allen Morris explained, "The Bryants feel they are not being unreasonable in insisting upon a measure of privacy, particularly to preserve the proper environment for two young daughters."

Bryant championed the cause of higher education. He guided the adoption of a constitutional amendment which allowed bond funding for the construction of universities and community colleges. Although he campaigned as a segregationist, as governor he permitted county school districts to integrate voluntarily.

Farris and Julia Bryant joined their three daughters, Julia, Cecilia, and Adair, in the mansion courtyard.

GOVERNOR

William Haydon Burns

&

FIRST LADY

Mildred Carlyon Burns

January 5, 1965 – January 3, 1967

Life at the mansion was often made chaotic by the joyous antics of the Burnses' visiting grandson. Little Clay, a toddler, was known for his boundless energy and curiosity, and once sent his eight-months-pregnant mother, Eleanor, diving into the pool fully dressed to retrieve him. Governor and Mrs. Burns decided it best to keep the little rover contained and turned the old dog run into a child's play yard, complete with a sandbox and swing set. The Highway Patrol and security men at the house made a comical sign which they posted in the back yard: "Beware of Boy."

Florida's thirty-fifth governor was born in Chicago in 1912. His parents, Harry and Ethel Burns, moved to Jacksonville when young William was ten years old. His college years took him to Wellesley, Massachusetts to attend Babson College, but he returned to Florida during the Great Depression, and managed to attain a state auditing job in Tallahassee. A few years later he moved again to Jacksonville and operated a variety of businesses: an appliance store, a plumbing company, a greeting card concern and a flying school. In 1934 he married "the girl next door," Mildred Carlyon, a young lady who had grown up on the same street as he. They raised two children, Eleanor and Bill.

During World War II, he used his pilot's license and knowledge of airplanes while serving in the U.S. Navy as an aeronautical salvage specialist with the Office of the Secretary. He obtained the rank of lieutenant. Burns first entered politics in 1949 in a successful bid for mayor of Jacksonville, an office he held for fifteen years. He championed massive public works programs and prompted businesses to locate in the city.

In 1964, in his second gubernatorial bid, Burns won the nomination of the Democratic Party. Relying on a competent organization headed by the "Burns Blitzers," he defeated Republican Charles R. Holley in the general election. A change in the state constitution the previous year shortened Burns's term to two years. Responding to growing voter support of Republican candidates in national races, Florida's predominantly Democratic leadership devised this strategy so that gubernatorial elections would move to nonpresidential election years.

After the November election, Governor and Mrs. Bryant proffered the soon-to-be first family an invitation to lunch and to view the mansion. "'It's

lovely,'" Mrs. Burns told a *Miami Herald* reporter. "'It's a little overwhelming, but it's lovely.'" For the first time since the Fuller Warren years, there would be no children residing at the home. The Burnses' son Bill was attending the University of Florida, and daughter Eleanor was busy with her husband, Lloyd Watkins, and two-year-old son, Clayton Burns Watkins. Preparing for the times when her children and grandchild would visit, Mr. Burns painted the upstairs bedrooms in appropriate colors explaining, "There's always room for a crib." She planned to keep the Jacksonville home they had lived in for twenty-six years fully equipped for visits and brought with her only personal items.

The Burnses soon gained a reputation for hosting elegant parties due in part to Mr. and Mrs. Parker Henderson, caterers who came from Jacksonville to serve as chefs in the Burns administration. Mrs. Burns devised a filing system for menus and guest lists, to ensure that guests would never be served the same meal twice. Mrs. Burns was, however, equally as comfortable in a blouse and slacks, participating in a bowling league, as in a formal gown. She was an avid gardener and made significant

In the reception room Governor and Mrs. Haydon Burns were joined by their visiting family: son Bill Burns on the left and daughter Eleanor Burns Watkins, with son-in-law Lloyd Watkins and grandson Clay.

An Associated Press wire photo showed Mildred Burns enjoying a favorite avocation. The caption read: "In spite of a very busy social schedule, Florida's first lady finds time to work in her flower garden at the Governor's Mansion."

improvments to the mansion grounds, for which she received the Garden of the Month Award from the local garden club. She also supervised the creation of a souvenir brochure about the mansion.

Governor Burns declared several of the homes surrounding the mansion "eyesores" and directed the state cabinet to purchase the properties to create a green space around the mansion. Together, Governor and Mrs. Burns also oversaw the replacement of the greenhouse used to raise plants for the residence and the capitol building. Terry Lee, a member of the Board of Commissioners for State Institutions, told the *St. Petersburg Times,* "The old greenhouse has completely gone to pot. It is not usable at all." The larger greenhouse was constructed on a vacant site south of the mansion.

At the end of his two-year "bob-tail" term, Governor Burns lost the race for the nomination of the Democratic Party, but was able to institute a variety of reforms during his brief tenure as chief executive. Massive growth in the state's revenues allowed for funding increases for the state parks system and for education. He sought to expand the state's manufacturing base and to establish strong trade ties with South America. He helped convince media giant Walt Disney Corporation to construct a theme park in central Florida. He proposed a $300 million plan to widen the state's highways with bond money, a strategy which was vigorously opposed and which helped propel Robert King High to front-runner status for the Democratic Party's nomination in 1966.

GOVERNOR

Claude Roy Kirk, Jr.

&

FIRST LADY

Erika Mattfield Kirk

January 3, 1967 – January 5, 1971

Dashing and flamboyant, Florida's first Republican governor since Reconstruction was dubbed "governor a go-go" by the Capital Press Corps.

Claude Roy Kirk was born in San Bernardino, California, in 1926. His parents, Claude Roy and Myrtle McClure Kirk, later moved to the Chicago, Illinois, area and then to Montgomery, Alabama. Kirk graduated from high school in Alabama's capital city and enlisted in the United States Marine Corps at the age of seventeen. During World War II he was decorated with the Air Medal and discharged as a first lieutenant. He returned to duty during the Korean conflict and became adept at jujitsu. Kirk received a B.S. degree from Duke University and then studied law at the University of Alabama. Polishing his salesmanship skills, he sold insurance and cofounded American Heritage Life Insurance Company in Jacksonville. He twice married and twice divorced Sarah Stokes, with whom he had four children, daughters Sarah and Katharine and twin sons William and Frank.

In 1960, Kirk switched his party alliance from Democrat to Republican and supported Richard M. Nixon's presidential campaign in the Sunshine State.

Four years later he was unsuccessful in a bid to unseat former governor and incumbent United States Senator Spessard Holland. In 1966 he was the Republican nominee for governor, defeating Miami Democrat Robert King High to become Florida's thirty-sixth governor.

Two months into office Kirk wed Erika Mattfield, a dazzling German-born divorcee from Brazil. He introduced her at the inaugural ball as "Madame X." Writing in the *Floridian,* Grace Bohne explained Mrs. Kirk's reception in the capital city: "Tallahassee … likes its first ladies on the ante bellum side, effusive, available, and — if nothing else — Democratic." The Kirks maintained dual residences during their tenure: the mansion and "Duck's Nest," their historic Palm Beach home.

Partisan politics brought the Adams Street house and its expenditures under intense scrutiny. The Kirks faced tough opposition for the most reasonable of requests. The *Tallahassee Democrat* reported that, "It cost $12.50 to have a sink unstopped by a local plumber." The Kirks meanwhile found

shortages in china for their entertaining needs and sought to supplement the collection. Mrs. Kirk was able to make a few changes to reflect her tastes. She planned a color scheme of olive green, yellow and orange ". . .to make the mansion more friendly and warm."

The household received an addition in August of 1968, when Mrs. Kirk gave birth to seven-pound, fifteen-ounce Claudia, named for her exuberant father. She was the first child born to a governor in office since 1907. Two years later the Kirks added a son, Erik Henry, to the first family.

As chief executive, Kirk made several inroads in a recalcitrant legislature. He supported reform efforts for the state's outdated 1885 constitution, resulting in a 1968 revision. He placed great emphasis on attracting new business to the state during his four-year term. He instituted a number of farsighted conservation reforms by founding the Water Pollution Control Commission, adding to publicly held lands and halting construction of the cross-Florida barge canal.

Claude Kirk announced at his inauguration: "The people will know who is governor, I am going to make things happen." With panache to spare, he quickly turned this declaration into an understatement.

Governor Claude Kirk wed German-born Erika Mattfield two months into his term on February 28, 1967. The marriage took place at the Breakers Hotel in Palm Beach, and the guest list at the reception included Republican presidential-hopeful Richard M. Nixon.

Reubin O'Donovan Askew

&

Donna Lou Harper Askew

January 5, 1971–January 2, 1979

Since childhood Askew yearned to serve in an elective office. He remembers, "Running for office was something I knew I had to do. …I feel God has plans for the world and men. If I had any talent I had to use it for public service."

Alberta O'Donovan Askew raised and educated her family as a single mother. Her carpenter husband, Leo Askew, left her in 1928 after the birth of her sixth child, who became Florida's thirty-seventh governor. Reubin Askew was born in Muskogee, Oklahoma, in 1928. In 1937 Mrs. Askew moved her children to Pensacola, where she supported her family working as a maid and seamstress.

Askew attended public schools in Escambia County. At the age of seventeen he enlisted in the army as a paratrooper and rose to the rank of sergeant. In 1948 he enrolled at Florida State University, where he earned a B.S. degree in public administration and was elected president of the student body. From 1951 to 1953, during the Korean conflict, he served in the air force with the rank of captain. After his discharge, the G.I. Bill enabled him to study law at the University of Florida, where he was president of his class and a member of the *Florida Law Review* staff.

In 1956 Reubin Askew wed Donna Lou Harper of Sanford. The couple took up residence in Pensacola, where he established a law practice and served as the assistant solicitor for Escambia County. Askew served twelve years as representative of his district in the state legislature: four years in the house of representatives and eight years in the senate. His peers elected him president pro tempore of the senate in 1969. Though barely known outside of his home county, Askew's friends convinced him to make a bid for the governor's office in 1970. Florida voters warmed to the sincerity of this public servant campaigning on a populist platform based on tax reform. As the nominee of the Democratic Party, he unseated incumbent Governor Claude Kirk with fifty-six percent of the vote. The revision of the constitution in 1968 provided that a governor could succeed himself for one four-year term. Askew's re-election in 1974 made him the first chief executive to serve two consecutive four-year terms.

Governor-elect and Mrs. Askew and their two children — Angela Adair and Kevin, aged nine and seven — moved into the governor's mansion two days prior to his inauguration. The youngsters were thrilled about their new home. A *United Press* reporter quoted Donna Lou Askew about the excitement of the children: "'I wish you could have seen them. They were in fairyland. They had such a good time running the elevator up and down.'"

The mood at the mansion changed from the pizzazz of the Kirk years to the more domestic lifestyle of the Askews. Accustomed to stronger drinks, one newspaperman was surprised when the governor offered apple juice during a mansion conference. *Time* magazine described Askew as a "nonsmoking teetotaler who devotes most of his spare time to the Presbyterian Church activities." Family was an equally important focus, with the governor especially encouraging his children in their interests — horse shows for Angela, bowling for Kevin, and scouting for both. After a new batch of guppies was born, Angela told a writer for the *Floridian* that "we have a total of 32 live animals here now."

During the Askew years, several additions were made to the grounds at the Adams Street property, among them a tennis court on the block south of the mansion. The addition of a new decorative security fence in 1973 was prompted in part by a visit to Tallahassee by Vice-President Spiro Agnew. When U.S. Secret Service officers surveyed the mansion in advance, they reported an unfavorable security assessment. Agnew chose to stay at the Holiday Inn instead.

The Askew years also saw a plan to create a "Governor's Park," which would provide a green buffer surrounding the residence and the adjoining property of the Grove. While the state did acquire some additional lots, funding was not provided for the entire property envisioned by the governor.

Mrs. Askew hosted a variety of occasions to open the mansion for visitors and wanted ". . .all Floridians to feel at home when they visit the executive residence." She enjoyed living with the fine antiques in the house and worked closely with the five-member Governor's Mansion Advisory Council. She invited James Cogar, originator of the interior design, to visit in 1972 and reported that he was pleased that the colonial revival plan had been maintained with integrity. Mrs. Askew and the advisory council began to refurbish the upholstery of state room furniture, which had begun to show eighteen years of use. Over the Askew years there were additions to the collections of mansion table linens, china and crystal.

Governor Askew devoted much of his first term to making Florida's tax structure more progressive. He campaigned for a constitutional amendment to allow a corporate income tax. Working with lawmakers he repealed

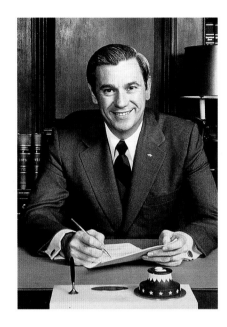

Governor Reubin Askew had previously spent twelve years in the state legislature. Among Florida voters he gained a reputation for sincerity and fair play.

Angela and Kevin Askew joined their parents in welcoming a visitor from the Magic Kingdom.

consumer taxes on utilities and apartment rentals and raised the homestead exemption. During his second term he fought for a variety of conservation measures, as well as the "Sunshine Amendment" requiring public officials to disclose their sources of income.

A champion of public education, he ardently supported integrated schools in Florida. Askew also dramatically increased the number of African-Americans serving in appointed offices. He nominated Joseph W. Hatchett to the Florida Supreme Court, the first African-American to serve on the court since Reconstruction. During the final months of his administration, he successfully rallied support against an amendment which would have legalized casino gambling in the state.

GOVERNOR

Daniel Robert Graham

&

FIRST LADY

Adele Khoury Graham

January 2, 1979–January 3, 1987

Mrs. Graham told the Fort Lauderdale News, *"'We're proud of the state home and we want to share it with as many people as possible and leave it even a more beautiful home than when we found it.'"*

Governor Bob Graham was born in Coral Gables in 1936. His father, Ernest Graham, moved to Dade County in 1919, where he founded a large dairy and cattle concern and later served as state senator from Dade County. Graham's mother, Hilda Simmons Graham, hailed from Walton County where she had been a school teacher. Graham grew up in a house built of coral rock in Pennsuco and attended public schools in Dade County. He graduated from the University of Florida in 1959 with a bachelor's degree and married Adele Khoury of Miami Springs that same year. The young couple moved to Massachusetts, where Graham graduated from Harvard University Law School, and then returned to south Florida where he became associated with the Graham family business.

Dade County voters gave him his first elected office, a seat in the Florida House of Representatives, in 1966. Four years later he was elected to the Florida Senate. After winning the 1978 governor's race, the Grahams moved from Dade County to the governor's mansion in 1979 with their four daughters: Gwen, Cissy, Suzanne, and Kendall.

Mrs. Graham brought a good deal of creative energy to the mansion. She instituted a program providing regularly scheduled public tours of the state rooms by volunteer docents. Also under her leadership, the Governor's Mansion Advisory Committee was upgraded to the Governor's Mansion Commission. To enhance the furnishings of the residence without spending public dollars, she founded the Governor's Mansion Foundation. During the eight years the Grahams resided in the house, the Foundation provided the funds for a number of large projects. Working with a design team, the Mansion Commission refurbished the state rooms, carefully preserving the spirit of the decor while making the mansion a more warm and gracious place. The Commission also approved the addition of the state Florida room, a Foundation-funded project which proved to be the harmonious conversion of an exterior patio into a valuable living space. The Commission hired a curator to care for the growing number of objects held

The Graham family gathered in the newly added Florida room. Clockwise from lower left: Cissy Graham, son-in-law Mark Logan, Gwen Logan, Kendall Graham, Suzanne Graham, Governor Bob Graham, and First Lady Adele Graham.

Midway through his first term Governor Bob Graham said, "Every day is a new challenge. I never had a more enjoyable twenty-three months."

in the public trust at the mansion. They also approved a thorough appraisal of the collection and saw that it was properly insured.

The Grahams hosted a variety of special events including Florida History Live, a living history celebration. President Jimmy Carter and other notable guests visited the mansion during their tenure. In June of 1985 the Grahams hosted a wedding reception in celebration of their daughter Gwen's marriage to Mark Logan. Some 700 well wishers came to the mansion on that occasion. Gwen, reflecting on the busy preparations, told Dorothy Clifford of the *Tallahassee Democrat:* "It's not been easy around here with the Legislature in session and re-doing the mansion. Even if you don't have anything else to do, planning a wedding can be pretty hectic."

As governor, Graham led the state through times of severe crisis, including the 1980 influx of Cuban-Haitian refugees, civil disturbances in Miami and a strike by truckers that threatened to paralyze the state. In 1979 two hurricanes threatened Florida back-to-back, and the governor oversaw massive evacuation programs and relief efforts. He continued a long interest in environmental matters and fostered a variety of proposals to protect Florida's ecosystems. The 1982 legislature approved his Save Our Rivers Act, which provided funding for the acquisition of river floodplains. Similarly, he approved the 1984 Wetlands Protection Act, which created five water management districts to protect the state's water supply. He supported Florida's law enforcement efforts and fought for federal assistance to combat crime.

Governor Graham was endeared to the citizens for his personal style of governing, and his "workdays" brought national attention. During his eight years as governor, Graham held over 180 "jobs," volunteering as a policeman, busboy, factory worker, teacher, newsman, social worker and even a sponge fisherman. ᕱ

GOVERNOR

John Wayne Mixson

&

FIRST LADY

Marjorie Grace Mixson

January 3, 1987–January 6, 1987

Florida Supreme Court Chief Justice Parker Lee McDonald adminis-tered the oath of office to Mixson on Saturday, January 3, 1987. Bringing his sense of humor to the inaugural, Mixson quoted Abraham Lincoln's "Gettysburg Address": "The world will little note nor long remember what we say here."

Florida's thirty-ninth governor served for just three days after succeed-ing Bob Graham, who resigned his office early to enter the United States Senate. Robert Martinez was already Florida's governor-elect. Wayne Mixson was born near New Brockton, Alabama, in 1922 on the farm of his parents, Cecil and Mineola Moseley Mixson. He moved to Panama City in 1941 and joined the navy, serving in a lighter-than-air unit. He attended Columbia University in New York and the University of Pennsylvania. In 1947 Mixson graduated with honors from the University of Florida Business Administration School. That same year he married Margie Grace of Graceville, Florida. The couple resided in Jackson County near Marianna and operated a 2,000-acre farm raising cattle, soybeans and peanuts.

Mixson held his first elected office, to the Florida House of Representatives, in 1967. He served in that body for six consecutive terms, becoming a strong advocate for Florida's rural communities, as well as working for the state's cities, students and industrial development. In his first statewide race in 1978, he joined Bob Graham as candidate for lieu-tenant governor on the Democratic Party ticket.

A privately funded reception at the old Capitol served as a festive end to his twenty years of public service. With a few changes of clothes, he and Mrs. Mixson set up temporary residence in the state guest bedroom of the gov-ernor's mansion so that they wouldn't interfere with workers who were readying the upstairs bedrooms for Governor-elect and Mrs. Martinez.

The brief tenure allowed for a cookout at the mansion for staff members. As a writer for the *Tallahassee Democrat* asked: "After all, what North Florida politician worth his hickory chips would let it be said that he got to be governor and didn't bother to have a barbecue at the mansion?" The Mixsons also invited the public to an open house at the residence after the inaugural festivities. Two nights later they packed their suitcases to make way for the Martinez family.

Wayne and Margie Mixson are shown here in the family stairway during their brief tenure as Florida's first family.

In his first statewide race, Robert Martinez ran, in 1986, as the Republican nominee for governor and won, becoming the first Florida governor of Hispanic descent since the colonial era and the second Republican since Reconstruction.

Bob Martinez was born in Tampa on Christmas Day in 1934. He was the only child of Spanish-Americans Serafin and Iva Martinez and the grandson of Spanish immigrants who moved to Tampa at the turn of the century. The future governor grew up in West Tampa where his father was a waiter at the renowned Columbia Restaurant in Ybor City. He attended Jefferson High School, lettering in basketball and baseball.

In 1954, a year after their high school graduation, Martinez married his high school sweetheart, Mary Jane Marino, and the young couple took turns putting each other through college. Martinez earned a bachelor of science degree in social science education from the University of Tampa and later a master's degree in labor and industrial relations from the University of Illinois.

Mary Jane Martinez worked as a dental assistant, eventually graduating from the University of South Florida with a bachelor's degree in library science and English. She began her career as a librarian at Tampa's King High School. The future governor taught American history, worked for the public teacher's union, and later became the owner and operator of Cafe Sevilla, a popular eatery where he cultivated political ties. Together, the couple reared two children, Robert Alan and Sharon Marie.

In 1979 Tampans elected Martinez mayor, a position he held for seven years. In 1986, in a well-organized campaign, the Republican mayor defeated his Democratic opponent to become Florida's fortieth governor.

Bob Martinez was Florida's first governor of Hispanic descent since the colonial era. Seven years as mayor of Tampa molded the leadership perspective he brought to the governor's office.

The Martinez family posed in the reception room. From left to right: daughter Sharon Keen holding Emily Ida, Bob Martinez, Mary Jane Martinez, son-in-law Neil Keen holding Lydia Marie, and son Alan Martinez.

Governor-elect and Mrs. Martinez visited the mansion prior to the inaugural to view their new home. Though their son and daughter were grown and had their own homes, the Martinezes planned to reappoint one of the upstairs bedrooms for their twin granddaughters, Emily Isa and Lydia Marie. Three months into her residency Mrs. Martinez told the *Florida Times-Union,* "'It's beginning to feel like home. We have a lot of our family portraits and we brought some of our things from Tampa, and I think that has helped in making it feel and look like home.'" They also brought with them the family's three-year-old basset hound, Tampa Mascotte, who, among other adventures, jumped into the presidential limousine when President Bush visited the mansion.

For her granddaughters, Mrs. Martinez added a swing set on the south lawn. The governor, who had been co-captain of his high school basketball team, enjoyed a new basketball goal that was placed behind the house. In a larger project, Mrs. Martinez worked with the Governor's Mansion Foundation to raise funding for a terraced patio with a fountain near the cabana building. The Martinez years saw the addition to the mansion grounds of *Manatee Dance,* a bronze sculpture by Hugh Nicholson, commemorating the state marine mammal. In addition to supervising the household and caring for her family, Mrs. Martinez worked throughout the state on a variety of volunteer efforts. As a former high school librarian, she focused much of her energy on working with teenagers, especially the youth in state facilities.

During his four-year tenure, Martinez effected a variety of reforms. He offered leadership on many environmental concerns including a systematic Solid Waste Disposal Act and Preservation 2000, a decade-long project to acquire sensitive lands for protection. The "War on Drugs" also became a Martinez issue, as he implemented federally recommended antidrug measures as well as championing the promotion of the "drug-free workplace." Confrontations with the legislature ultimately led to state budget-making

reforms, which Martinez supported. He brought attention and action to issues such as offshore oil-drilling and the construction of more prisons. He won bipartisan support for SWIM, creating for the first time a series of uniform policies for the management and protection of Florida's surface waters. As Florida continued to become more of a two-party state, the governor sought to strengthen and build the Republican Party.

GOVERNOR

Lawton Mainor Chiles, Jr.

&

FIRST LADY

Rhea Grafton Chiles

January 8, 1991–

During the Chiles years, the mansion has hosted a number of national and international political leaders, ambassadors, foreign ministers, authors, and scientists. In 1995 President Clinton came for dinner and an overnight stay in the state guest room. He requested salsa and nacho chips for snacks and was served a Florida cracker favorite: fresh pan fried mullet with grits for breakfast.

Florida's forty-first governor is a third-generation Floridian born on April 3, 1930 in Lakeland, the son of Lawton Chiles, a railroad conductor, and Margaret Patterson Chiles, daughter of a pioneer Florida family who settled the city of Auburndale. His great-grandfather was a field surgeon in the Confederate army. While attending the University of Florida Law

School, Chiles married his college sweetheart, Rhea Grafton. He returned home from military service in Korea and was admitted into the Florida Bar in 1955. He practiced law in his hometown where the couple raised their four children: Tandy, Bud, Ed, and Rhea.

Chiles got his first taste of political experience serving as speaker pro tempore at Boys' State and driving a car for Fuller Warren in his campaign for governor. His first run for public office was a successful 1958 door-to-door campaign in which he and Rhea knocked on 350 doors a day in Polk County. He unseated a veteran legislator to win a seat in the Florida legislature, where he served for the next twelve years. Late in 1969, Chiles entered a nine man race for the United States Senate seat vacated by Spessard Holland. With scant statewide recognition and even less funding, he expanded on his Polk County door-to-door campaign and walked the entire length of Florida. Beginning in the spring of 1970, he covered 1,003 miles in ninety-two days. The tactic earned him the nickname "Walkin' Lawton." He won — defeating former Governor Farris Bryant in the run off. Chiles won two more elections to the United States Senate, always voluntarily limiting his campaign contributions to $100. A writer for *Time* magazine said Chiles "typified the historic and fundamental Southern notion of populism; defending the little man, attacking the Establishment."

In Washington in 1973, Rhea Chiles founded Florida House, located directly behind the United States Supreme Court. Restored and renovated by contributions from the private sector, Florida House provides information and hospitality to Floridians visiting the nation's capital. She was the recipient of the 1981 Annual Award of the Florida Trust for Historic Preservation.

Visiting for the holidays, the Chiles family gathered outside the mansion. From left to right, beginning with the front row: Geoffrey Chiles, Ashley Chiles, Katie Chiles, Brynne MacKinnon, Lawton Chiles IV, Mack MacKinnon, Tandy Barrett, Christin Chiles; standing: Anne Chiles, Ed Chiles, Bud Chiles, Kitty Chiles, Bo Barrett, Rhea Chiles, Lawton Chiles, Tandy Chiles Barrett, Alex MacKinnon, Rhea Chiles MacKinnon, Annesley MacKinnon, and Joe Lawton Barrett.

In 1990, Chiles defeated incumbent governor Martinez. When the Chileses moved into the governor's mansion in January of 1991, they brought a legacy of nearly forty years of service to the state of Florida. Reflecting on the holiday season in the executive residence, Rhea Chiles said, "Family Christmas at the mansion is a story book experience. The house is filled with beautiful decorations and flowers, and our grandchildren are so excited about being at the mansion for the holiday."

During the Chiles years the mansion kitchen was renovated and the mansion park landscaped with plantings indigenous to Florida. Administrative improvements included a computerized inventory scan auditing system of mansion furnishings, and electronic linkage between the governor's capitol office and the mansion. The curator's office was moved from another state building into an office in the mansion.

As governor, Chiles has championed legislative reforms to increase the affordability of health care for children in the prenatal and early childhood years. In the aftermath of Hurricane Andrew in 1993, the state emergency center was upgraded to the most effective in the country. Chiles secured $300 million in federal funding for Florida's Preservation 2000 program. Under his leadership Florida became the first state to sue tobacco companies for smoking related damages to the health of Floridians, for which the state had been paying $440 million dollars annually. He advocated the prevention of crime through programs for early intervention in the lives of disadvantaged youths.

Following his second successful bid for the governor's office, Lawton Chiles thanked voters outside the Old Capitol.

RIGHT: In March 1995 President Clinton addressed the joint session of the Florida Legislature and stayed overnight at the governor's mansion. Here he relaxes with Governor Chiles and sons Bud and Ed Chiles.

CKNOWLEDGEMENTS

The members of the Florida Governor's Mansion Foundation wish to thank the following individuals for the generous donation of their time and talents.

Jill Alford	Dianne Maxwell	Trish Pierce
Debra Benton	Jo Miglino	Scotty Sanderson
Bob Broward	Joan Morris	Michelle A. Scalera
Brittany Clark	Richard Nichols	Jeanine Slagle
Hillary Clark	Dixie L. Nims	Christopher Still
Jerome Cummings	Joanna Norman	Dan Stengle
Bruce Groetz	Steve Orpallo	Dana Strickland
Kelly Kimsey	Elizabeth Outlaw	Cindy Tomas
Gene Leedy	Robert Overton	Eric Tourney
Debbie Leonard	Karen Pankowski	Jim Towey
Rhea Chiles MacKinnon	Gayle Penner	Annie B. Williams
Leon Martin		Lynn Wurtz

The members of the Florida Governor's Mansion Foundation gratefully acknowledge these corporate contributors.

Lithohaus Printers, Inc.

The Little Communications Company

Presstek, Inc.

Ron Sachs Communications

Vanessa B. Zein-Eldin

Zimmerman Agency

SELECTED BIBLIOGRAPHY

Carper, N. Gordon. "Martin Tabert, Martyr of an Era." *Florida Historical Quarterly* 52 (October 1973): 115-131.

Colburn, David R. and Richard K. Scher. *Florida's Gubernatorial Politics in the Twentieth Century.* Tallahassee: University Presses of Florida, 1980.

Cox, Merlin G. "David Sholtz: New Deal Governor of Florida." *Florida Historical Quarterly* 43 (October 1964): 142-152.

Drane, A. Hank. *Historic Governors: … Their Impact on the Sunshine State.* Ocala, Florida: Ferguson Printing, 1994.

Flynt, J. Wayne. *Cracker Messiah: Governor Sidney J. Catts of Florida.* Baton Rouge: Louisiana State University Press, 1977.

Gannon, Michael. *Florida: A Short History.* Gainesville: University Press of Florida, 1993.

McDonell, Victoria H. "Rise of the 'Businessman's Politician': The 1924 Florida Gubernatorial Race." *Florida Historical Quarterly* 52 (July 1973):39-50.

Mendez, Armando. *Ciudad de Cigars: West Tampa.* Tampa: Florida Historical Society, 1994.

Morris, Allen. *The Florida Handbook: 1993-1994.* 24th Biennial ed. Tallahassee, Florida: Peninsular Publishing Company, 1993.

Poesch, Jessie. *The Art of the Old South: Painting, Sculpture, Architecture & the Products of Craftsmen.* 1989. Reprint. New York: Harrison House, 1983.

Proby, Kathryn Hall. *Audubon in Florida.* Coral Gables, Florida: University of Miami Press, 1974.

Proctor, Samuel. *Napoleon Bonaparte Broward: Florida's Fighting Democrat.* 1993. Reprint. Gainesville: University Press of Florida, 1950.

MANUSCRIPT COLLECTIONS

LeRoy Collins Papers, University of South Florida Library

Governor's Mansion Commission Papers, Florida State Archives

Spessard Holland Papers, University of Florida

Frank D. Moor Papers, Florida State University

Park Trammell Papers, University of Florida

Napoleon B. Broward Papers, University of Florida

ARCHIVAL PHOTOGRAPHY

The following photographs appear through the courtesy of the following collections:

Florida State Archives: *Pages 8, 15, 16, 18, 19, 21, 22, 23, 24, 25, 27, 28, 29, 31, 33, 44, 74, 90, 100, 102, 104, 106, 107, 112, 114, 115, 117, 118, 120, 121, 122, 123, 124, 125, 126, 127, 128, 131, 133, 135, 137.* The British Library: *Page 14.* The Museum of Florida History: *Pages 15, 75.* The State Library, Florida Room Collection: *Pages 16, 17, 102, 104.* LeRoy Collins Leon County Public Library: *Page 26.* The Historical Society of Palm Beach County: *Page 29.* Preservation Foundation of Palm Beach: *Page 30.* Mrs. Nell Carlile: *Page 31.* The John & Mable Ringling Museum of Art: *Pages 47, 60.* College of William & Mary, Swem Library: *Page 50.* University of South Florida Library, Special Collections: *Page 53.* Cornell University, Carl A. Kroch Library: *Page 54.* Abby Aldrich Rockefeller Folk Art Center, Williamsburg, VA: *Page 54.* New York Historical Society: *Page 60.* Florida Division of Tourism: *Pages 72, 73, 75, 90, 140.* Governor's Mansion Collection: *Pages 68, 69, 74.* Mrs. Susan Caldwell Cavanagh: *Page 119.* Mrs. Eleanor Burns Watkins: *Page 129.* Mrs. Adele Graham: *Page 135.* Mrs. Margie Mixson: *Page 136.* Lois D. Griffin, Griffin Gallery: *Page 137.* Mrs. Rhea Chiles: *Pages 139, 140.*